Exploring Fossils: An Activity Book

Written and Illustrated by Jasper Burns

Edited by Susan B. Felker, Dr. Nicholas Fraser, Dr. Lauck Ward.
Activities by Jasper Burns, Eileen Merritt, and Sonya Wolen.
Design and Layout by Lisa Perrell

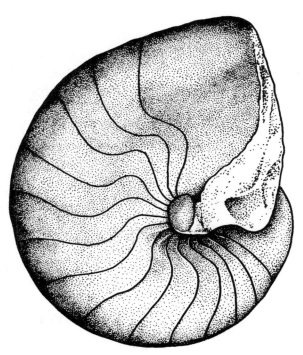

This publication is made possible by a grant from
the Martinsville Rotary Club

Virginia Museum of Natural History
1001 Douglas Avenue
Martinsville, VA 24112
Internet: http//www.vmnh.org

Chapter 1—
How are fossils formed?

In most cases, when a plant or animal dies, its remains are soon destroyed. Wind, rain, sun, waves, and underwater currents cause dead plants and animals to decay. Scavengers feed on them. Forces of nature also obliterate most other traces of past life, such as burrows, tracks, or the cast-off leaves of plants. In order to be preserved as fossils, dead plants and animals must be protected from the elements quickly. **Sediments**, which include the mud and sand that accumulate at the bottom of bodies of water, often protect dead plants and animals from destruction. Fossils of animals and plants that live in or near water are relatively common for this reason. Wind-blown sediments, which are known as **aeolian deposits**, sometimes bury and preserve fossils as well.

Remains or traces of dead organisms that have been successfully buried may still be destroyed by bacteria, burrowing animals, or erosion. Acidic water may dissolve the remains, leaving cavities known as **molds** in the sediments. These molds may then be filled with mineral deposits, forming **casts** that take on the original shape of the animal or plant that was buried. In other cases, the plant or animal matter is replaced gradually by rock-hard minerals. This process, called permineralization, preserves even internal structures. Petrified wood often forms in this way.

Nature preserves fossils in other ways. For example, at the La Brea Tar Pits in California, tar preserved many prehistoric animals including **mammoths** and saber-toothed tigers. In the coldest regions of the earth, ice or frozen soil buried some prehistoric animals and plants and preserved them for thousands of years. In other places, animals died in caves or in crevices where their skeletons were safe from scavengers or exposure to the weather.

These fossils may be further protected by burial under sediments that accumulated in the caves.

The Mid-Atlantic region has no tar pits full of fossils, nor year-round ice fields, but it does have an abundance of sedimentary deposits that accumulated in seas and at the bottoms of lakes and rivers. These sediments buried and protected the traces and remains of many living things and contain fossils that are reminders of the life and landscapes of the past.

In some rock exposures, you can see the sand and mud of ancient seas and lakes exposed on dry land in the form of **sedimentary rocks** such as sandstone and shale. The sediments have been turned into rock by pressure and by chemical processes. In the same way, accumulations of shells turned into rock known as limestone. However, in the Coastal Plain, much of the sand and mud deposits never turned into rock at all. Fossils of prehistoric animals and plants may be found in these sediments, protected from destruction for millions of years.

On very rare occasions, the original markings and colors of fossils are preserved. But we have no way to be sure that these colors have not been altered by time. We have no record at all of how most prehistoric animals were marked. This means that the colors you see in books and on television of dinosaurs and prehistoric fish are the result of speculation. Artists make educated guesses based largely on comparison with the appearance of living plants and animals, or they use their imagination in recreating the past for the audience. As you color the creatures in this book, consider the factors that influence the colors and markings of living things today.

Lasting Impressions

Fossils are created in nature when the remains of plants or animals are preserved by being buried in sediment. Often, the actual shells, bones, or leaves dissolve, leaving cavities in the sediments called molds. Molds may later be filled with mineral deposits, forming casts that take on the original shape of what was buried. You can make a mold and a cast of a shell or leaf to simulate how some fossils form.

Materials:

Plaster of Paris	Cup
Vaseline	Paper
Water	Shells or leaves
Spoon	Paint (optional)

Small plastic dish or the bottom of a milk carton
Soft clay (natural clay works well)

1. Choose a shell or leaf. Flatten the clay to make a "pancake" slightly larger and thicker than the shell or leaf.
2. Gently rub a little vaseline over the shell or leaf. Press the part of the shell or leaf with the most detail into the clay. Carefully remove the shell or leaf. You should see an impression, or mold, in the clay.
3. Mix the plaster of Paris in the cup with enough water to make a very thick liquid. Place the clay mold in the plastic dish. Pour the plaster into the mold and let it harden overnight.
4. The next day, carefully pull the clay away from the plaster of Paris. You should have a cast of the shell or leaf.
5. You can paint the cast, but remember that fossils rarely show the colors of the original shell or leaf.

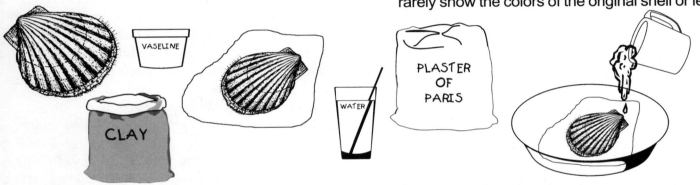

Against All Odds

Scientists have to work hard to find and identify fossils. It seems like there is an endless supply, but it is actually unusual for plant or animal remains to survive over millions of years. When a plant or animal dies, very special conditions have to be present for fossil preservation. This experiment will help you begin to understand some of the difficulties faced in the process of preservation.

Materials:
Three slices of bread
Two cups of sand
Two quart size jars with lids
Two paper towels
Water

1. Fold each paper towel in half and in half again, so each one is about the size of a piece of bread.
2. Wet one paper towel with water and place it in the bottom of one of the jars.
3. Put one slice of bread on top of the wet paper towel, then close the lid tightly.
4. Put another slice of bread in the second jar. Pour the sand on top of it, making sure it is completely covered, then close the lid tightly.
5. Set both jars outside.
6. Place the second paper towel on the ground next to the jars. Put the third slice of bread on top of it.
7. Check on the bread every day for a week. Create a chart to track what you see happening to each slice of bread (without opening the jars).
8. At the end of the week, open the jars. What differences do you see between the slices of bread?
9. Which slice do you think would have made the best fossil? Why?

Clocks in the Rocks

Every day we use a clock to keep track of time— time for school, time for lunch, time for bed. Geologists and paleontologists use other clues to keep track of long spans of time. They use the rocks! Rocks can't tell the time of day, but they can tell us the order in which things happened.

Try to make a list of the clothes you wore over the past week.

Yesterday	Two days ago
Three days ago	Four days ago

Now, check out the laundry basket or clothes hamper. The things you wore yesterday will probably be on top. The clothes from the day before are under those, etc. If you count the daily layers of clothes, you can tell how long it has been since anyone did the laundry. If you find dress-up clothing in the layers it tells you a special event may have happened that day.

This is similar to the way scientists look at layers of rock in a cliff face. The layers help them understand how much time has passed and when specific geologic events happened. Most importantly, it provides a record of relative time. The layers on top represent more recent events; what is below them are older events, getting more and more ancient as you move down the face of the cliff.

Chapter 2
How old are fossils?

People often describe fossils and prehistoric life, as being "millions of years old." But how do scientists know how old fossils are? Scientists first determine the age of the rocks or sediments in which fossils are found. This is done by analyzing the amounts of radioactive elements that occur in the deposits or in the fossils themselves, such as mollusks, which contain strontium.

Using this and other methods, scientists have estimated that the Earth formed four billion, six hundred million years ago! The oldest fossils ever found—of microscopic **bacteria**-like marine organisms—are more than three billion, five hundred million years old! The oldest fossils found in North America are "only" about seven hundred million years old. These fossils, called **stromatolites,** are structures built by algae and bacteria.

Other than stromatolites, most early fossils are poorly preserved remains of softbodied animals like worms and jellyfish, and soft, water-dwelling plants like **algae**. These fossils are rare because soft remains are much less likely to be preserved than hard objects like shells or bones. Around 570 million years ago, sea animals began forming shells that were more easily fossilized.

Scientists who study fossils, called paleontologists, discovered that different kinds of fossils are found in different ages of rocks depending on what plants and animals existed when the rocks formed. For example, the remains of dinosaurs may only be found in rocks that are less than 230 million years old but more than 65 million years old. Using this information, paleontologists have divided the history of life on earth. The largest division of geologic time is known as an era. An era is divided into periods which are further divided into epochs.

AGE MILLION YEARS AGO	ERA		PERIOD		EPOCH
	CENOZOIC	QUAT.	NEOGENE		HOLOCENE
					PLEISTOCENE
5—		TERTIARY			PLIOCENE
					MIOCENE
25—			PALEOGENE		OLIGOCENE
					EOCENE
					PALEOCENE
65—	MESOZOIC		CRETACEOUS		
150—			JURASSIC		
210—			TRIASSIC		
250—	PALEOZOIC		PERMIAN		
300—			CARBONIFEROUS	PENNSYLVANIAN	
350—				MISSISSIPPIAN	
400—			DEVONIAN		
			SILURIAN		
450—			ORDOVICIAN		
			CAMBRIAN		
570—			PRE–CAMBRIAN		
4600—					

The oldest rocks with numerous fossils come from the Paleozoic Era, which means "the era of ancient life." The Paleozoic Era began 570 million years ago when shells first appeared. The next large division of geologic time is called the Mesozoic Era, which means "the era of middle life." It began 248 million years ago and is also known as "the age of dinosaurs." The latest major division of earth history is the Cenozoic Era, meaning "the era of recent life." This era began 65 million years ago when dinosaurs became extinct and continues to the present day.

The time chart shows the divisions of geologic time. Many names of time periods come from places where rocks of their age are plentiful. For example, rocks of the Pennsylvanian Period are very common and available for study in the State of Pennsylvania. Most of the period names are from places in Europe. Notice that the time before the beginning of the fossil-rich Paleozoic Era, called "Pre-Cambrian Era" in our chart, is more than four billion years long, or more than 80% of the earth's history!

Chapter 3
What can we learn from fossils?

There are many reasons for collecting and studying fossils. Many fossils are beautiful and all are interesting to study. Hunting for them can be lots of fun and discovering the remains of a plant or animal that died millions of years ago is a great thrill. It is hard to imagine that you are the very first person to see something that has been hidden for so long.

One of the best reasons to study fossils is to learn about the history of life on earth. This helps us to understand the present. Because each age of sedimentary deposit has its own particular kinds of fossils, we can see how certain kinds of plants and animals have become **extinct** while others have taken their places. By describing and comparing fossils from around the world, scientists have been able to piece together many parts of the puzzle of how life has changed through time. We can even follow the changes within a single group of plants or animals. By studying the fossils of one particular type, it is possible to trace how they developed, or changed, through time. For example, we can see how the prehistoric ancestors of horses became larger and came to have fewer and fewer toes as time passed.

Fossils have also provided important clues about how the earth itself has changed. Paleontologists noticed that they found very similar kinds of shell fossils in rocks from the Devonian Period in the Appalachian Mountains of the eastern United States, in parts of Europe, and in the mountains of Morocco in North Africa. At first, this was very confusing. How could the same kinds of animals have lived so far apart when the modern sea animals from these parts of the world are so different? Eventually, using these fossils and other clues, the scientists realized that, during the Devonian Period, Africa, North America, and Europe were much closer together than they are today!

Chapter 4
Where can fossils be found?

Fossils are found in sedimentary rocks and deposits. Rocks of this type are very common and contain fossils of many kinds and ages. There are two other major types of rocks which rarely contain fossils. These are known as **igneous** rocks and **metamorphic** rocks.

Igneous rocks were formed from extremely hot molten material, such as magma, which is a liquid form of rock that comes from far beneath the earth's surface. Obviously, no plants or animals could live near this material, and if their remains came in contact with it, they would usually be destroyed. Metamorphic rocks are rocks that have been changed in their internal structure by extreme heat or pressure. They may have been either igneous or sedimentary rocks before this happened. If a metamorphic rock was originally a sedimentary rock that contained fossils, those fossils are usually destroyed or very badly damaged by the change.

The first step in looking for fossils is to find an area where the ancient sediments and sedimentary rocks are present. Then you must locate an **exposure**—a place where these deposits come to the surface. In most places, sedimentary rocks are covered by vegetation and a thick layer of soil. The best places to collect fossils are where erosion, roads, or quarries have cut through the soil and exposed the fossil-bearing sediments underneath.

You may need tools to collect fossils. A rock hammer and chisel can be used to break open hard sedimentary rocks to reveal the fossils inside. In softer deposits, a pick axe can scrape through the clay and sand to expose shells and animal teeth. Sometimes, fossils have already been freed from the deposits in which they were buried for so long, and all you have to do is pick them up.

Mapping Rocks

Use the map on the cover of this book to discover the ages and types of rocks that can be found in Virginia. Take this map along as you travel to help you locate areas where interesting fossils might be found.

Look for the metamorphic and igneous rocks on the map. They are mostly in the Piedmont and Blue Ridge. Many of these rocks were probably formed when a chain of volcanic islands collided with North America about 500 million years ago. Many of the igneous rocks were the roots of ancient volcanoes. Others were part of Africa hundreds of millions of years ago. All of these rocks were folded during the collision of continents. Scientists are uncertain of the ages of some of these rocks, since they have changed so much over time. These rocks are colored red on the map to remind you of the heat involved in the formation of igneous and metamorphic rocks.

Now find the sedimentary rocks west of the igneous rocks on the map. Many of these old rocks were deposited when water covered much of the land west of the Blue Ridge Mountains. These Paleozoic, sedimentary rocks are colored blue on the map to remind you of the water that used to cover the land. If you want to find very old fossils such as crinoids and trilobites, look in these rocks.

Look carefully to locate the sedimentary rocks from the Mesozoic Era. They can be found in scattered areas, often surrounded by metamorphic and igneous rocks. These sediments collected in rift valleys when North America and Africa were breaking apart, and the Atlantic Ocean was beginning to open up. If you want to find fossils from the age of the dinosaurs, you need to look in these rocks and sediments. These rocks are colored green on the map to remind you of the lush plants that were abundant during the Mesozoic.

Furthest east on the map, you will find the most recent sedimentary rocks and sediments. They contain creatures similar to the animals we see today. Some of these fossils are found in sediments that are still loose and haven't been formed into rocks yet. The color yellow was used for these Cenozoic sediments and sedimentary rocks to remind you of the sand where fossils may be found.

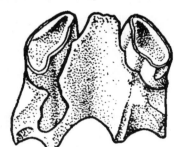

GROUND SLOTH—
JAW FRAGMENT WITH TWO TEETH

BEAR CANINE
TOOTH
URSUS

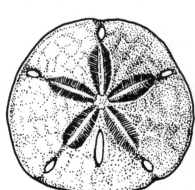

ECHINOID—MELLITA

Chapter 5 The many kinds of fossils.

Some of the more recent fossils you are likely to find, especially from the Cenozoic Era, may look familiar. There are clams, sand dollars, and conch shells in these sediments which look a great deal like those you find at the beach. You will not recognize many of the fossil plants and animals that occur in deposits of all ages, and especially in the much older Paleozoic rocks.

There are two main types of animals. These are **vertebrates** and **invertebrates**. Vertebrates are animals that have backbones, such as fish, amphibians, reptiles, birds, and mammals. Invertebrate animals do not have backbones and include snails, clams, insects, corals, and starfish. Invertebrates are either soft-bodied or have external skeletons of shells.

Many mollusks have shells that are readily preserved as fossils. Some kinds of mollusks are **bivalves**, like clams; **gastropods**, or snails; **scaphopods**, or tusk shells; and **cephalopods,** which include the shell-bearing **nautiloids** as well as squids and octopuses, which do not have shells.

Another group of invertebrate animals often found as fossils are the **brachiopods**. Brachiopods resemble clams because they have two shells which fit tightly together, but they are different from clams in many other ways. Brachiopods are **marine** animals which are not common in today's oceans but were very numerous during the Paleozoic Era. Their fossils are abundant in Paleozoic rocks.

A great variety of invertebrate animals belong to the group known as **arthropods**. Insects, barnacles, crabs, and centipedes are some of the types of arthropods living today whose fossil remains may be found. **Trilobites** are extinct ocean-dwelling arthropods which disappeared from the Earth about 250 million years ago. Their fossils are often discovered in the Paleozoic sedimentary rocks in the Appalachian Plateau and Valley and Ridge areas.

The invertebrate marine animals known as **echinoderms** include starfish and sand dollars. Other echinoderms, often found as fossils in Paleozoic rocks, are known as **crinoids, blastoids**, and **cystoids**. Most of these three types of animals have a rounded body attached to the bottom of the sea by a long, thin, flexible stem made up of many small round plates. Cystoids and blastoids have become extinct but crinoids still live today.

Other invertebrate animals whose remains may be found as fossils include the **bryozoans** and corals. Bryozoans form lacy, branching, or encrusting **colonies**. These structures are homes made by many individual bryozoans. Fossil corals can be found as colonies or as solitary forms. Both bryozoans and corals are common as fossils and still exist today. Less common are fossils of some extinct marine invertebrates such as **archaeocyathids, tentaculitids, hyolithids**, and **graptolites**. Because there are no living members of these groups of animals for comparison, it is difficult to know exactly how they lived.

Most of the species of plants and animals that are found as fossils are now extinct, and some whole groups of organisms—like trilobites and dinosaurs—have disappeared.

Other living things, such as **Cycads**, which have very similar living relatives, are unfamiliar to us because they live today only in other parts of the world. Cycad fossils are common in the Cretaceous. They still live in parts of eastern Asia, California, Australia, southern Africa, and Central America. Because they no longer live anywhere near the Mid-Atlantic region, the presence of cycad fossils may be puzzling to us but their fossils are evidence of their earlier distribution.

PLACOPECTEN

CAMBRIAN—TRILOBITE—KOOTENIA

CAMBRIAN—
HYOLITHID

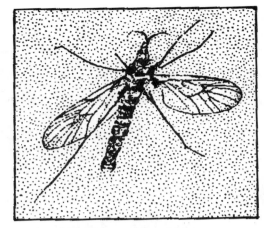

TRIASSIC—FLY FOSSIL

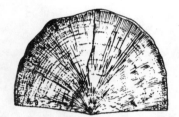

ORDOVICIAN—BRACHIOPOD—
RAFINESQUINA

About Scientific Names

Because scientists come from many parts of the world and speak many languages, they need a standard system for naming plants and animals which they all can understand. They spell out the names using Latin, the language spoken in ancient Rome, because no one speaks it anymore and it does not change. Scientific names for the plants and animals preserved as fossils are often listed under their pictures throughout this book. The text sometimes lists the name of the rock **formation**, abbreviated FM., where the fossil was found.

CAMBRIAN—
TRILOBITE

CRETACEOUS—
PINE CONE—
CONUS VERMENSIS

TRIASSIC—
DOSWELLIA

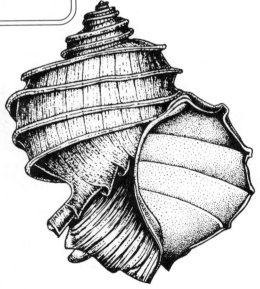

PLIOCENE—
GASTROPOD—
ECPHORA
QUADRICOSTATA

Puzzling Over Pangaea

Why do we think that six continents were joined into one supercontinent, called Pangaea, in the late Paleozoic Era? Scientists started noticing there was a pattern in the rock and fossil records of that time period. The fossils and rock types found in the eastern portion of North America matched nicely with those in the western portions of Europe and Africa. How did that happen? Try to make the connection. Copy (or trace) and cut out the six continents below. How would you fit them together into one supercontinent?

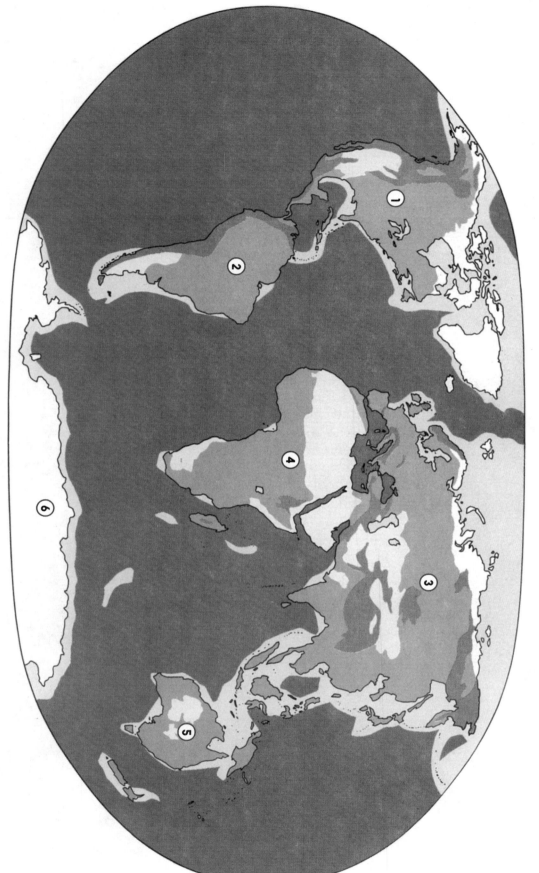

See page 26 for answer map.

12

CAMBRIAN—ROME—FM.—
TRILOBITE—PTYCHOPARELLA

CAMBRIAN—SHADY FM.—
GASTROPOD—HELCIONELLA

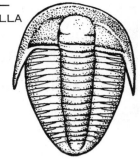

During most of the Paleozoic Era, the continental crust which now forms this region was divided into two parts. One was part of the continent of North America. The other—what is now the eastern section—was part of the continent of Africa! There are a few, poorly preserved fossils from the Paleozoic age in the formerly African portion, now in the piedmont, but the Appalachian mountains and valleys hold a fabulous fossil treasure from this time. This part of North America was at or near the Equator during the Paleozoic Era, so its fossils are of tropical plants and animals.

Fossils from the earlier periods of the Paleozoic—the Cambrian, Ordovician, Silurian, Devonian, and Mississippian Periods—are mostly marine in origin. This is because most of the Mid-Atlantic region was covered by warm, shallow seas during those times. The seas receded from the land in the later Paleozoic. Most sedimentary rocks from the Pennsylvanian Period in the eastern United States contain fossils of animals and plants that lived in swamps and forests.

By the Permian Period, the last period in the Paleozoic Era, all of Virginia was above sea level. For this reason, very few sediments accumulated. There are no sedimentary rocks of this age in Virginia today. However, Permian rocks in neighboring West Virginia and Pennsylvania give a good idea of the kinds of plants and animals that lived in the area.

One important event of the late Paleozoic was the collision of North America with Africa and Eurasia. These three continents, plus Australia, South America, and Antarctica, joined together in one vast supercontinent, which is known today as Pangaea. In the early Mesozoic Era, Pangaea began to split apart into the separate continents we see today. It was at this time that a piece of the original Africa stayed with North America.

In the following pages, you will see pictures of plant and animal fossils from the Paleozoic Era. Also shown are scenes of how the organisms might have appeared when they were alive. Remember that many of these kinds of living things have been extinct for millions of years. No one knows exactly what they looked like or how they lived. By studying their closest living relatives, and by noticing details of the fossils and how and where they were buried, we can make some educated guesses about what the ancient worlds of the Paleozoic looked like.

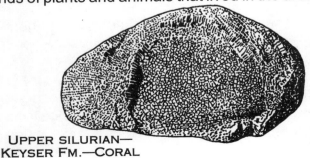

UPPER SILURIAN—
KEYSER FM.—CORAL

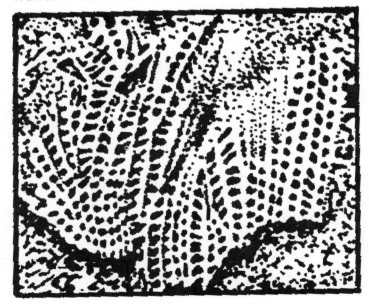

BRYOZOAN—SEPTOPORA

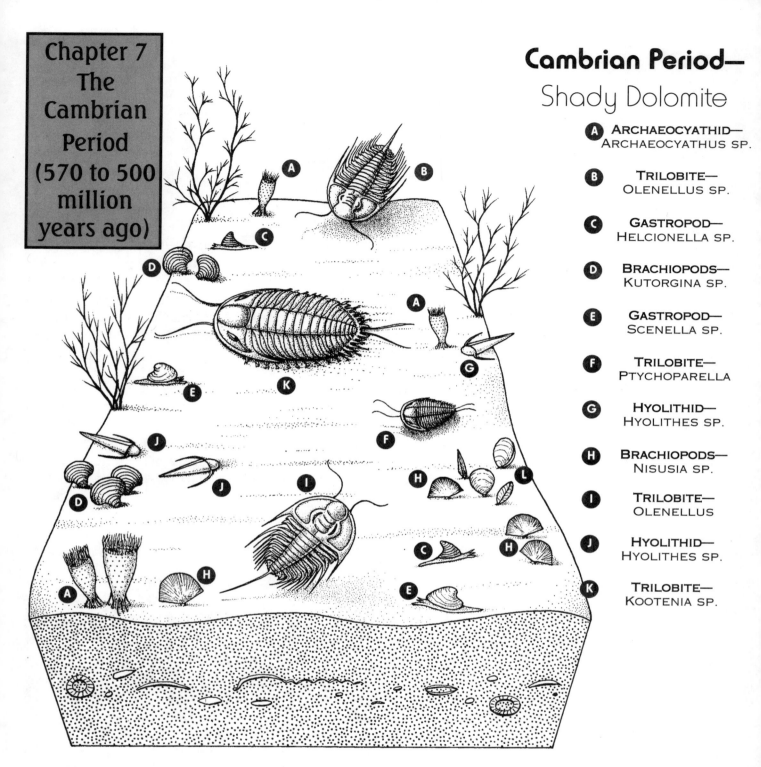

Chapter 7
The
Cambrian
Period
(570 to 500
million
years ago)

Cambrian Period—
Shady Dolomite

A ARCHAEOCYATHID—
ARCHAEOCYATHUS SP.

B TRILOBITE—
OLENELLUS SP.

C GASTROPOD—
HELCIONELLA SP.

D BRACHIOPODS—
KUTORGINA SP.

E GASTROPOD—
SCENELLA SP.

F TRILOBITE—
PTYCHOPARELLA

G HYOLITHID—
HYOLITHES SP.

H BRACHIOPODS—
NISUSIA SP.

I TRILOBITE—
OLENELLUS

J HYOLITHID—
HYOLITHES SP.

K TRILOBITE—
KOOTENIA SP.

During the Cambrian Period, the Mid-Atlantic region was home to many of the first sea animals with hard shells. These included brachiopods, gastropods or snails, and especially trilobites. Other extinct marine animals such as archaeocyathids and hyolithids are preserved as fossils in Cambrian rocks. Stromatolites may also be found in some of these deposits. These structures, made by a kind of marine blue-green algae that uses the energy of sunlight in a way similar to plants, are still forming today on the coast of Australia.

The illustration above shows a Cambrian sea-floor community of plants and animals that once lived in the warm, shallow seas of the mid-Atlantic region.

Chapter 8
The Ordovician Period (500 to 438 million years ago)

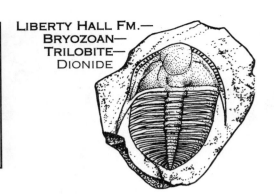

LIBERTY HALL FM.—
BRYOZOAN—
TRILOBITE—
DIONIDE

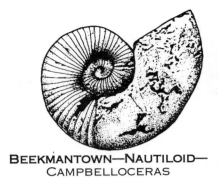

BEEKMANTOWN—NAUTILOID—
CAMPBELLOCERAS

During the Ordovician Period, the seas became home to more diverse marine life. Trilobites were still very common. Many new kinds of brachiopods and mollusks such as gastropods (snails), bivalves (clams), and nautiloids were abundant. Nautiloids belong to the class of mollusks known as cephalopods. The modern squid and octopus also belong to this group, as does the only kind of nautiloid that lives today—the so-called "pearly Nautilus"—which has a coiled shell. During the Ordovician, many nautiloids grew long, straight, cone-shaped shells, while others grew the familiar coiled form. All had shells which were divided into chambers like the living Nautilus.

Other interesting sea animals whose fossils are common in Ordovician rocks are corals, crinoids, cystoids, bryozoans, sponges, and graptolites. Graptolites were colonial animals, meaning that many individuals built a common structure in which to live. They were extremely common in the Ordovician Period, but less so in later times. They became extinct during the Devonian Period. Fish swam in the Ordovician seas, but their fossils are rare throughout the Paleozoic.

The reconstruction opposite shows a representative community of animals that lived on a muddy bottom in an Ordovician sea.

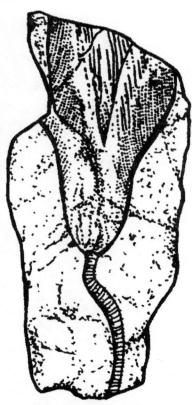

MARTINSBURG FM.—
CRINOID

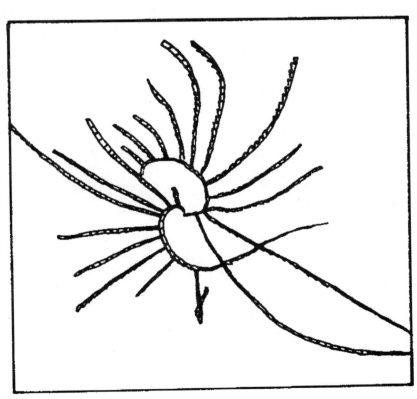

GRAPTOLITE—
NEMAGRAPTUS

Ordovican Period—
Martinsburg Formation

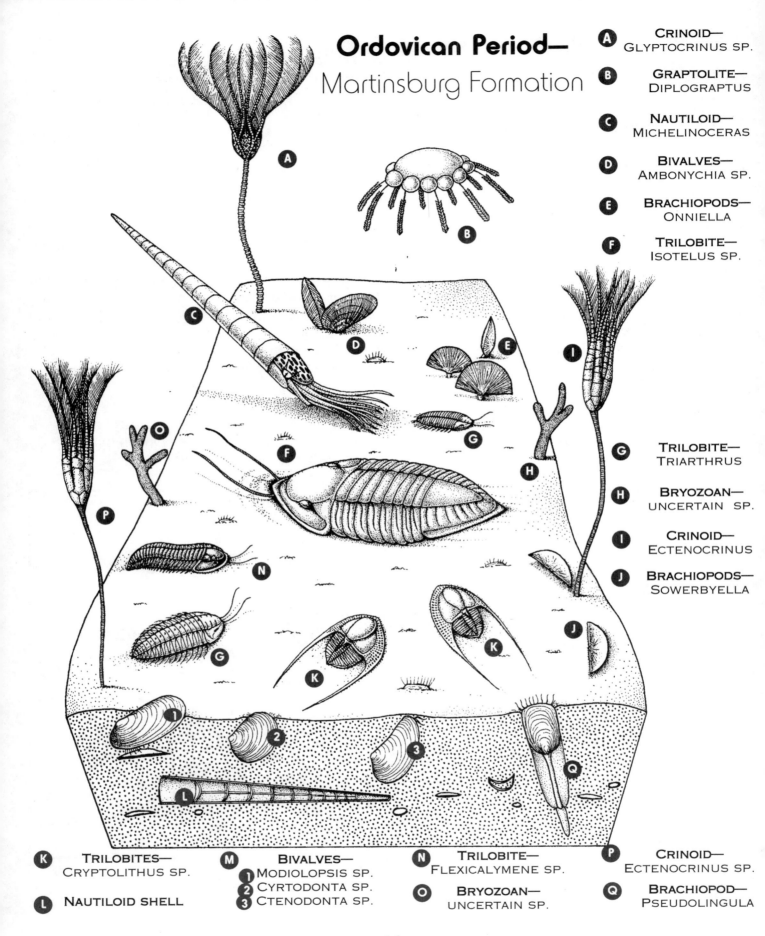

A CRINOID—
GLYPTOCRINUS SP.

B GRAPTOLITE—
DIPLOGRAPTUS

C NAUTILOID—
MICHELINOCERAS

D BIVALVES—
AMBONYCHIA SP.

E BRACHIOPODS—
ONNIELLA

F TRILOBITE—
ISOTELUS SP.

G TRILOBITE—
TRIARTHRUS

H BRYOZOAN—
UNCERTAIN SP.

I CRINOID—
ECTENOCRINUS

J BRACHIOPODS—
SOWERBYELLA

K TRILOBITES—
CRYPTOLITHUS SP.

L NAUTILOID SHELL

M BIVALVES—
1 MODIOLOPSIS SP.
2 CYRTODONTA SP.
3 CTENODONTA SP.

N TRILOBITE—
FLEXICALYMENE SP.

O BRYOZOAN—
UNCERTAIN SP.

P CRINOID—
ECTENOCRINUS SP.

Q BRACHIOPOD—
PSEUDOLINGULA

Silurian rocks from the Mid-Atlantic contain fossils very similar to those found in Ordovician rocks.

Trilobites, brachiopods, gastropods, bryozoans, cystoids, crinoids, sponges, and nautiloids were still abundant and varied. Corals are especially common in Silurian limestones. Some are fairly large individual animals called **'horn corals'** because of their horn-shaped skeletons. Other corals formed colonies consisting of many tiny individuals, known as **corallites**, each living in a separate hole in a stony structure.

Some typical Silurian Fossils

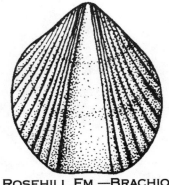

ROSEHILL FM.—BRACHIOPOD
HOMOEOSPIRA

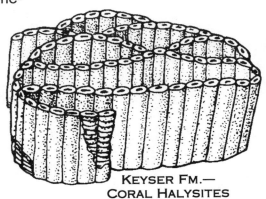

KEYSER FM.—
CORAL HALYSITES

KEYSER FM.—BRACHIOPOD
CUPULAROSTRUM

WILLS CREEK FM.—
BIVALVE—
PTERINEA

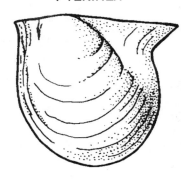

ROSEHILL FM.—TRILOBITE
LIOCALYMENE

KEYSER FM.—BRYOZOAN—
FENESTELLA

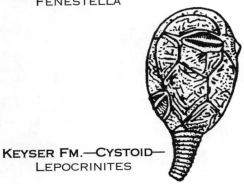

KEYSER FM.—CYSTOID—
LEPOCRINITES

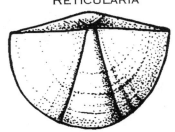

ROSEHILL FM.—BRACHIOPOD—
RETICULARIA

ROSEHILL FM.—BRACHIOPOD
CHONETES

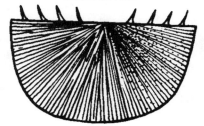

Silurian Period—
Keyser Formation

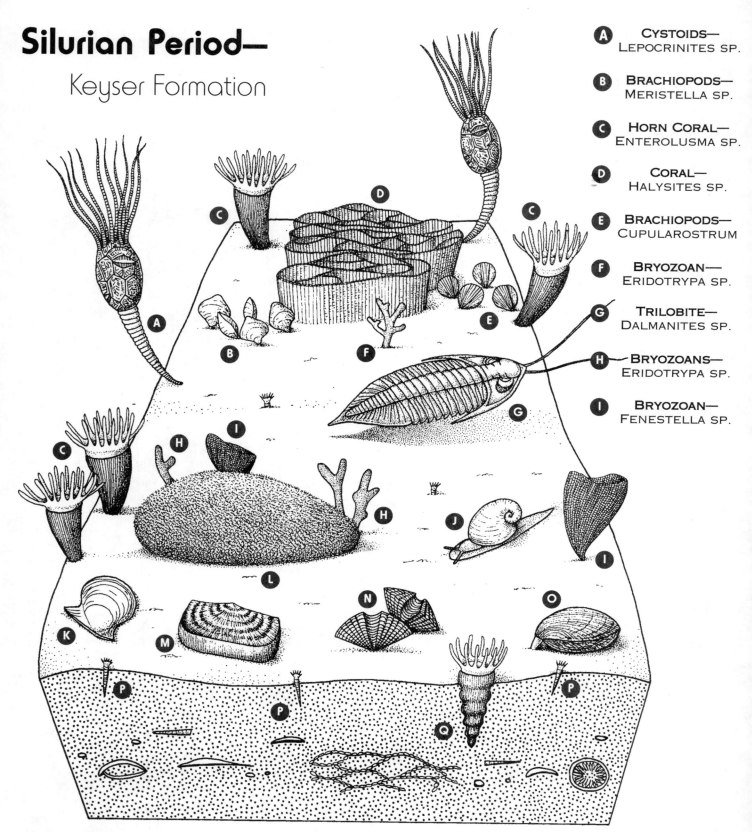

A CYSTOIDS—
LEPOCRINITES SP.

B BRACHIOPODS—
MERISTELLA SP.

C HORN CORAL—
ENTEROLUSMA SP.

D CORAL—
HALYSITES SP.

E BRACHIOPODS—
CUPULAROSTRUM

F BRYOZOAN—
ERIDOTRYPA SP.

G TRILOBITE—
DALMANITES SP.

H BRYOZOANS—
ERIDOTRYPA SP.

I BRYOZOAN—
FENESTELLA SP.

J GASTROPOD—
PLATYCERAS SP.

K BIVALVE—
PTERINEA SP.

L CORAL—
FAVOSITES SP.

M BRACHIOPOD—
LEPTAENA SP.

N BRACHIOPOD—
CYRTINA

O BRACHIOPOD—
ATRYPA SP.

P TENTACULITIDS—
TENTACULITES SP.

Q "HORN" CORAL—
UNCERTAIN SPECIES

18

The Devonian Period fossil record is extensive. Trilobites, crinoids, corals, bryozoans, and nautiloids remained very common. New types of cephalopods known as ammonoids, which were very similar in appearance to nautiloids, also appeared. Perhaps the most distinctive fossils from this time are the brachiopods, especially the kind known as **spiriferids**. These animals had a distinctive hump, or fold, in the middle of their shells and a series of rib-like ridges on either side of the fold. Though present since the Ordovician Period, the spiriferids became especially large, varied, and abundant during the Devonian. Their fossils are very common in Mid-Atlantic states.

It was during the Devonian that land plants first formed primitive forests. These forests were home to animals such as centipedes, scorpions, and the first amphibians, which evolved from air-breathing fish. Fossils of plants from these Devonian forests are occasionally found in Virginia.

Typical Devonian Fossils

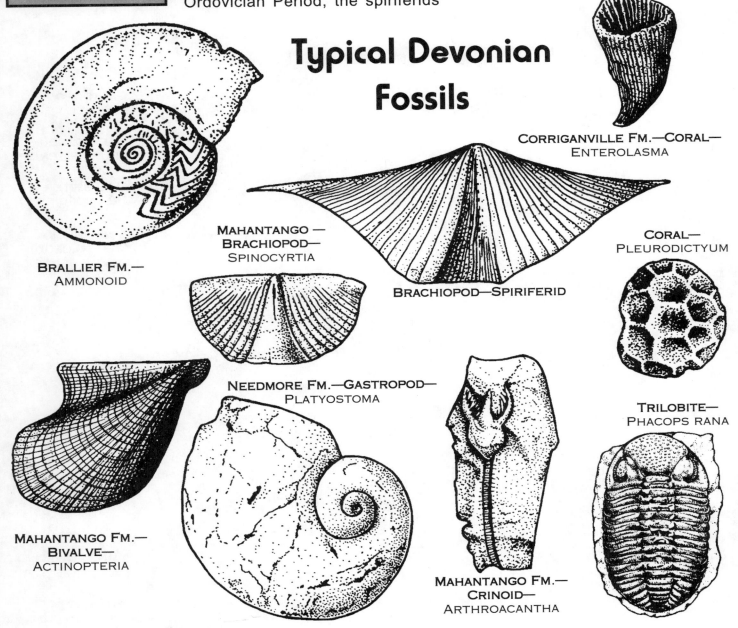

CORRIGANVILLE FM.—CORAL—
ENTEROLASMA

BRALLIER FM.—
AMMONOID

MAHANTANGO —
BRACHIOPOD—
SPINOCYRTIA

BRACHIOPOD—SPIRIFERID

CORAL—
PLEURODICTYUM

NEEDMORE FM.—GASTROPOD—
PLATYOSTOMA

TRILOBITE—
PHACOPS RANA

MAHANTANGO FM.—
BIVALVE—
ACTINOPTERIA

MAHANTANGO FM.—
CRINOID—
ARTHROACANTHA

Devonian Marine Life

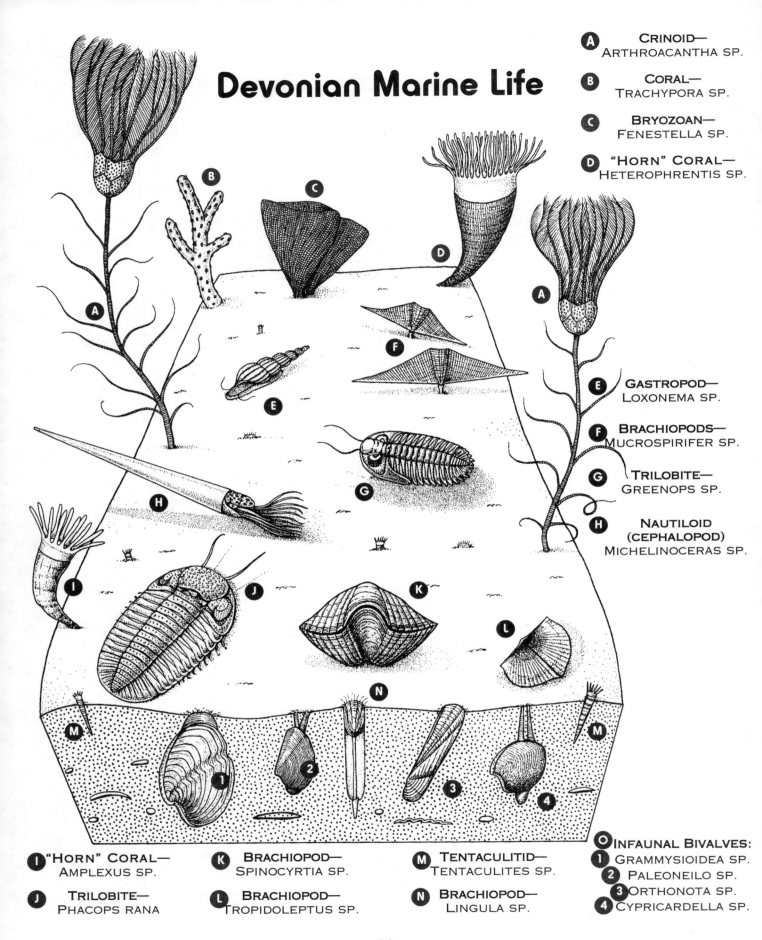

A CRINOID—
ARTHROACANTHA SP.

B CORAL—
TRACHYPORA SP.

C BRYOZOAN—
FENESTELLA SP.

D "HORN" CORAL—
HETEROPHRENTIS SP.

E GASTROPOD—
LOXONEMA SP.

F BRACHIOPODS—
MUCROSPIRIFER SP.

G TRILOBITE—
GREENOPS SP.

H NAUTILOID
(CEPHALOPOD)
MICHELINOCERAS SP.

I "HORN" CORAL—
AMPLEXUS SP.

J TRILOBITE—
PHACOPS RANA

K BRACHIOPOD—
SPINOCYRTIA SP.

L BRACHIOPOD—
TROPIDOLEPTUS SP.

M TENTACULITID—
TENTACULITES SP.

N BRACHIOPOD—
LINGULA SP.

O INFAUNAL BIVALVES:
1 GRAMMYSIOIDEA SP.
2 PALEONEILO SP.
3 ORTHONOTA SP.
4 CYPRICARDELLA SP.

20

Chapter 11
The
Mississippian
Period
360 to 320
million years ago

Limestones from the Mississippian Period contain an abundance of brachiopods, corals, bryozoans, crinoids, and blastoids. Blastoids, like crinoids, were attached to the sea bottom by long stalks made up of numerous small round plates. Trilobites were still present in Mississippian seas, but they were much less common and disappeared completely before the end of the Paleozoic Era.

Other kinds of fossils of Mississippian age are the remains of land plants. These specimens come from forests which flourished near the ancient coastline. Very rare footprints of amphibians that lived in these forests have been found in Virginia.

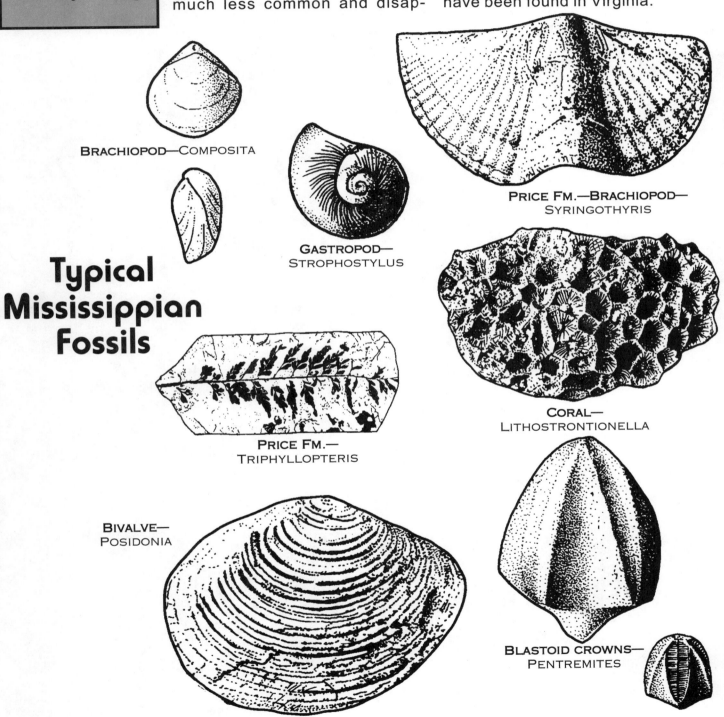

Typical Mississippian Fossils

BRACHIOPOD—COMPOSITA

GASTROPOD—
STROPHOSTYLUS

PRICE FM.—BRACHIOPOD—
SYRINGOTHYRIS

PRICE FM.—
TRIPHYLLOPTERIS

CORAL—
LITHOSTRONTIONELLA

BIVALVE—
POSIDONIA

BLASTOID CROWNS—
PENTREMITES

Mississippian Period

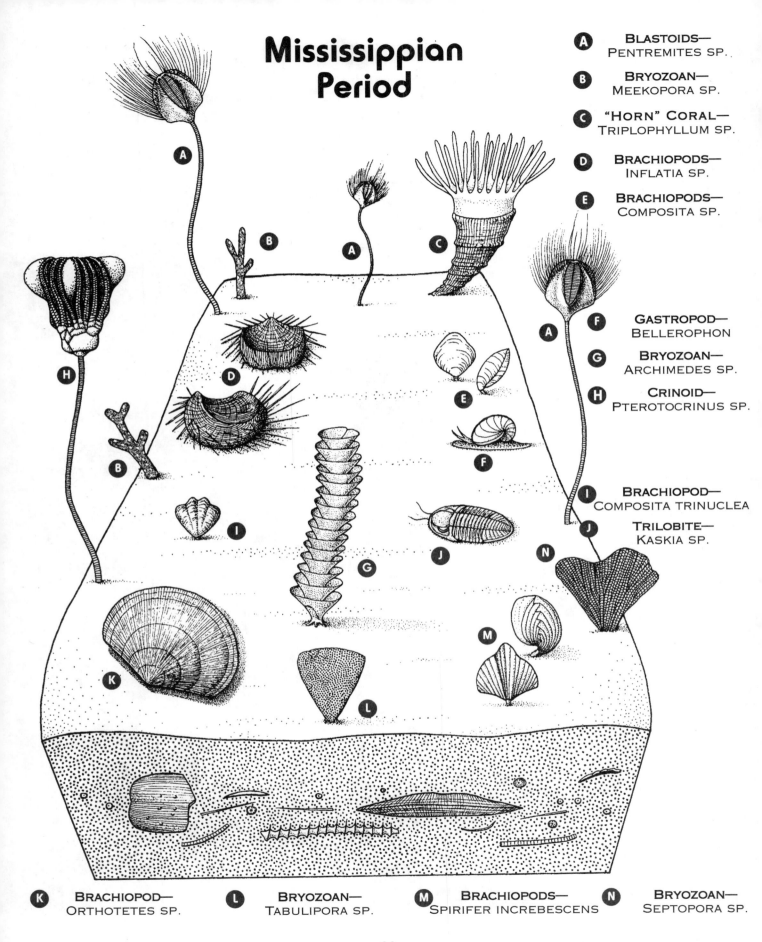

A BLASTOIDS— PENTREMITES SP.

B BRYOZOAN— MEEKOPORA SP.

C "HORN" CORAL— TRIPLOPHYLLUM SP.

D BRACHIOPODS— INFLATIA SP.

E BRACHIOPODS— COMPOSITA SP.

F GASTROPOD— BELLEROPHON

G BRYOZOAN— ARCHIMEDES SP.

H CRINOID— PTEROTOCRINUS SP.

I BRACHIOPOD— COMPOSITA TRINUCLEA

J TRILOBITE— KASKIA SP.

K BRACHIOPOD— ORTHOTETES SP.

L BRYOZOAN— TABULIPORA SP.

M BRACHIOPODS— SPIRIFER INCREBESCENS

N BRYOZOAN— SEPTOPORA SP.

22

Typical Pennsylvanian Plant Fossils

WISE FM.—SEED FERN
ALETHOPTERIS LONCHITICA

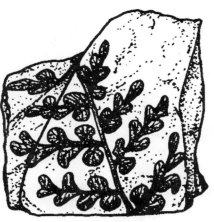

SEED FERN—
MARIOPTERIS

LEE FM.—SEED FERN
NEUROPTERIS POCAHONTAS

WISE FM.—HORSETAIL—
ASTEROPHYLLITES
EQUISTIFORMIS

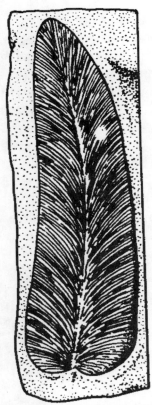

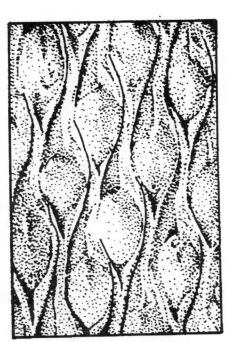

ARBORESCENT LYCOPOD—
LEPIDODENDRON

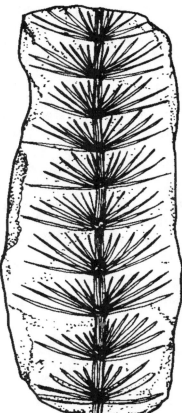

WISE FM.—SEED FERN
NEUROPTERIS SCHEUCHZERI

HORSETAIL—
CALAMITES (PITH CAST)

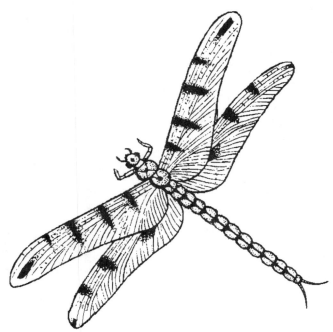

Chapter 12
The Pennsylvania Period and Permian Period
320 to 296 million years ago

In the last two periods of the Paleozoic Era, most of the Mid-Atlantic region was no longer covered by shallow seas. As the continents of North America, Africa, and Eurasia collided with one another, mountain ranges were created and the land in general became higher. The ocean waters receded. Almost all of the region's fossil-bearing rocks contain the remains of the plants and animals that lived on the land in forests or in the swamps and rivers nearby.

The Pennsylvanian forests were home to animals such as insects, centipedes, amphibians, and early reptiles. The swamps and rivers contained a variety of fish. The most abundant fossils from this time are of the spectacular plants that lived here. These included the segmented plants known as **horsetails**. One type of horsetail, named *Calamites*, grew to nearly 100 feet in height. The **scale trees**, a kind of **lycopsid**, towered as high as 150 feet! Also common were **true ferns** and **seed ferns**. Both of these kinds of plants often have leaves consisting of many tiny leaflets, but they are different

because true ferns use spores rather than seeds to reproduce. All of these plants were so abundant that their remains accumulated in thick layers. These deposits were then buried under sand and mud and gradually turned into coal. Many of the region's coal deposits formed from the remains of Pennsylvanian forests. (Other coal deposits date from the Devonian, Mississippian, and Triassic periods.)

There are no sedimentary rocks from the Permian Period in Virginia. Whatever sediments might have accumulated have since been eroded away. For this period, one must look at the fossil record in other areas. The Permian age rocks of West Virginia and Pennsylvania contain many of the same sorts of fossils as are found in the Pennsylvanian rocks.

Coal Forest of the Pennsylvanian Period

A	SCALE TREE— LEPIDODENDRON SP.	D	HORSETAIL— CALAMITES SP.	G	CENTIPEDE
B	TRUE FERN— PECOPTERIS SP.	E	SCALE TREE— SIGILLARIA SP.	H	SEED FERN— NEUROPTERIS SP.
C	COCKROACH—STENODICTYA	F	AMPHIBIANS— LABYRINTHODONTS	I	DRAGONFLY— MEGANEURON

Living Together

One of the many clues fossils hold is the story of their environment. By examining all the plants and animals that were living at the same time, scientists can make some educated guesses about ancient climates, predator/prey relationships, and food webs. Now, it's your turn to try.

Make a list of the wild plants and animals that live in your town. Think about the different kinds of birds and insects you see each day. Are there any mammals? Is there a stream, river, lake, or ocean near you? How does that body of water affect your list? What are the relationships between items on your list?

Visit your library in order to make a list of wild plants and animals that live in Africa. Do any of these living things match the ones on your neighborhood list? Do any of the relationships overlap?

Look at the list on this page. Can you make an educated guess about where these plants and animals might live together? What clues are in the list that help you guess?

Arctic fox
Grizzly bear
Moose
Musk ox
Wolf
Bald eagle
Boreal chickadee
Cliff swallow
Green-winged teal
Stilt sandpiper

Indian pipe
Northern windflower
Quaking aspen
Western hemlock
White spruce

Brain Alert!!

What will future scientists think if they find animal and plant fossils at a site that used to be one of our zoos? They might find the bones of lions next to those of polar bears. By moving animals around, do you think we may confuse the fossil records of the future? How many of the things that are alive today do you think might be preserved in the fossil record?

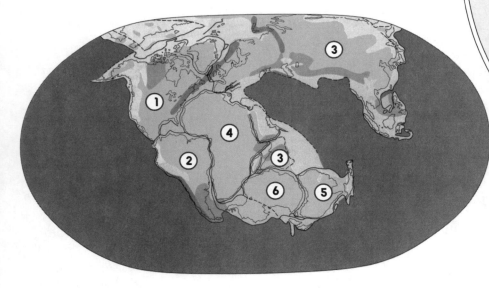

Puzzling over Pangaea answer for page 12.

Typical Triassic and Jurassic Fossils

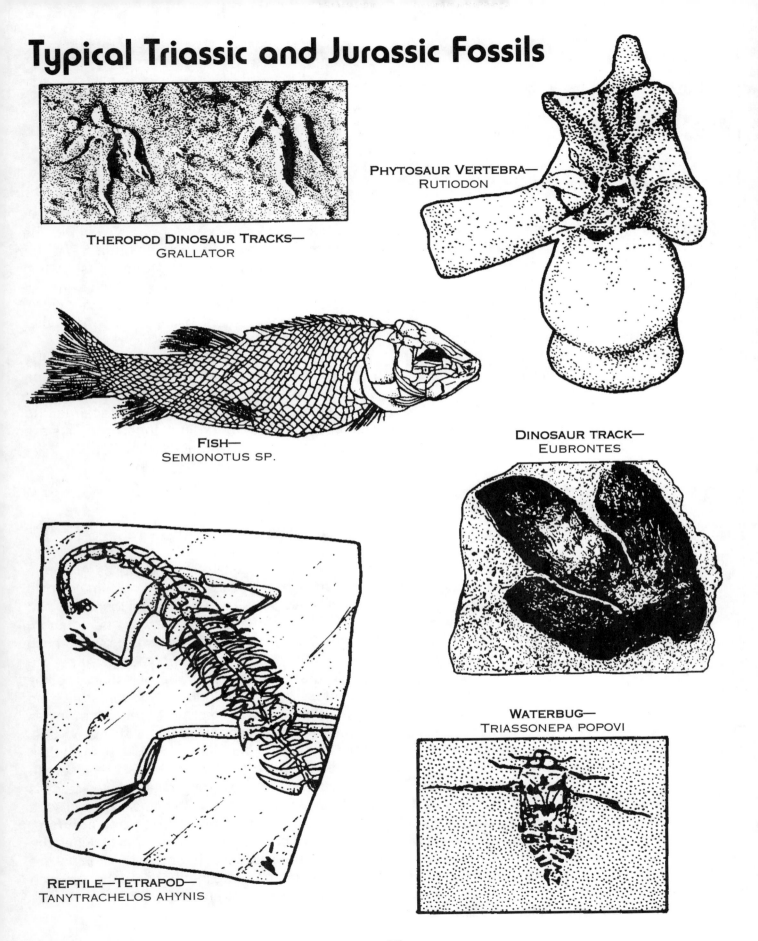

THEROPOD DINOSAUR TRACKS—
GRALLATOR

PHYTOSAUR VERTEBRA—
RUTIODON

FISH—
SEMIONOTUS SP.

DINOSAUR TRACK—
EUBRONTES

WATERBUG—
TRIASSONEPA POPOVI

REPTILE—TETRAPOD—
TANYTRACHELOS AHYNIS

27

Chapter 13
Fossils and Prehistoric Life
The Mesozoic Era

By the end of the Paleozoic Era, all of the Earth's continents had joined to form one land mass—the supercontinent known as Pangaea. The area we now call North and South Carolina was at the center of this land mass, near the Equator. In the beginning of the Mesozoic Era, the Triassic Period, Pangaea began to break apart into several continents. The earliest sign of this breakup occurred in what is now the eastern United States, as Africa and North America began to separate. The Atlantic Ocean eventually evolved between the continents.

When Africa and North America began to break apart, cracks appeared in the Earth's crust called "rifts." These rifts created low-lying areas or valleys where lakes and rivers formed. Over time, the sediments that collected in these bodies of water hardened into rocks that preserve a fascinating record of the life of the late Triassic and early Jurassic periods. By the Cretaceous Period, North America had moved north of the Equator. The other continents were slowly moving toward their present positions. On the Coastal Plain, bordering the Paleo-Atlantic ocean, there were lush forests on large river deltas which were home to dinosaurs of many kinds. Marine deposits of Cretaceous age also accumulated. In Virginia, these deposits are deeply buried under younger sediments.

Chapter 14
The Triassic and Jurassic Periods
248 to 144 million years ago

Late Triassic and early Jurassic fossils, which are preserved in rift valley sediments in the Piedmont, are extremely varied and important for what they tell us about the development of life on Earth. For example, Virginia has a greater variety of Triassic insect fossils than any other place in North America. Among these are the remains of beetles, flies, waterbugs, grasshoppers, and cockroaches.

A great deal has also been learned by studying reptile fossils from this time. Dinosaur tracks are not uncommon. Some of them were probably made by a species similar to the small meat-eating **theropod** dinosaur known as *Syntarsus*. The fossilized bones of some large Triassic reptiles have also been discovered. One of these reptiles, named *Doswellia*, had an armor-plated body. Also, the remains of a crocodile-like **phytosaur** were uncovered during construction at Dulles Airport in northern Virginia. Fossils of a relatively small reptile named *Tanytrachelos*, which had a long neck and tail, have been found in New Jersey and southern Virginia. It is believed that *Tanytrachelos* spent much of its time in the water and ate insects. The **cynodonts** are another group of extinct reptiles whose fossils may be found. Cynodonts are also known as "mammal-like reptiles" because their bones and teeth resemble those of mammals in many ways. Virginia's Triassic and Jurassic rocks also contain numerous fossils of freshwater fish, often preserved in such a way that the arrangement of the scales is still visible. Plant fossils from this time consist of seed ferns, true ferns, horsetails, cycads, and **conifers**, (the group of cone-bearing plants that includes the pines). In some areas, these plant remains are extensive enough to have formed coal deposits which have been commercially mined.

Triassic Freshwater Life

A TRUE FERN
B CYCAD
C REPTILE— TANYTRACHELOS

D WATERBUG (BELOSTOMATID)
E FLY (DIPTERAN)

F BEETLE (COLEOPTERAN)
G "GRASSHOPPER" (ORTHOPTERAN)

H DIVING BEETLE
I FISH— SEMIONOTUS SP.

Typical Cretaceous Plant Fossils

A CEPHALOTAXOPSIS

B FRENELOPSIS

C SEQUOIA CONE—POTOMAC FM.

D BAIEROPSIS

E OSMUNDA

PINE CONE—
CONUS VERMENSIS

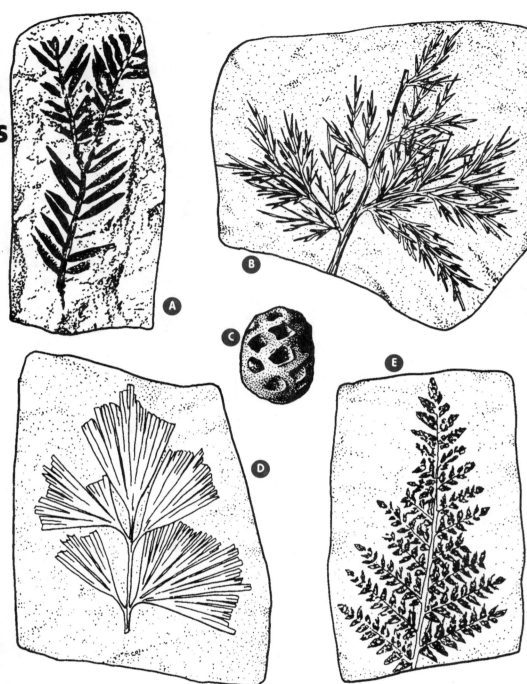

Chapter 15
Cretaceous Period
143 to 65 million years ago

Cretaceous fossils from Virginia consist primarily of the remains of land plants, including cycads, seed ferns, a species of **Sequoia** related to modern redwoods, horsetails, and conifers of many kinds. Occasionally, fish fossils and fossils of some freshwater arthropods known as crustaceans have also been found. Some fossils are found in amber in New Jersey. Numerous dinosaur fossils have been found in similar deposits in North Carolina and Maryland.

Virginia's marine sediments of Cretaceous age are completely covered by a thick accumulation of younger deposits. Numerous fossils of Cretaceous sea life may be found in neighboring states and in deep wells that are dug in some parts of Virginia.

Terrestrial Life of the Early Cretaceous

A COELURUS SP.

B BRACHIOSAURID—
  PLEUROCOELUS

C CYCADS

D ALLOSAURUS SP.

E PRICONODON SP.

F CYCAD

31

Typical Paleocene Fossils

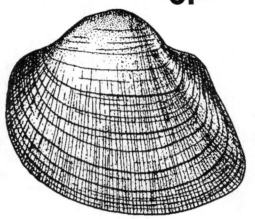

AQUIA FM.—BIVALVE—
CUCULLEA GIGANTEA

AQUIA FM.—CORAL—
BALANOPHYLLIA ELABORATA

AQUIA FM.—RAY TEETH—
MYLIOBATIS

CROCODILE TOOTH—
THECACHAMPSA

AQUIA FM.—
TURRITELLA MORTONI

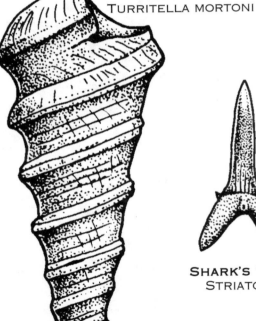

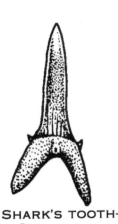

SHARK'S TOOTH—
STRIATOLAMIA

AQUIA FM.—INTERNAL MOLD—
TURRITELLA SP.

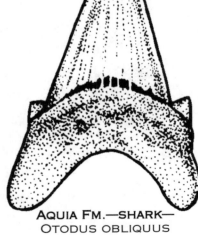

AQUIA FM.—SHARK—
OTODUS OBLIQUUS

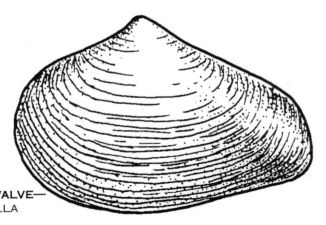

AQUIA FM.—BIVALVE—
CRASSATELLA

Chapter 16
Fossils and Prehistoric Life in Virginia
The Cenozoic Era

The Coastal Plain marine fossils of the eastern United States make up one of the most varied, abundant, and well-preserved records of past life found anywhere in the world. Fossils of mollusks, vertebrates, corals, bryozoans, echinoderms, and many other animals representing both of the Cenozoic periods and all seven of its epochs are found. These Cenozoic fossils are the first abundant fossils of sea life to be preserved in Virginia since the Mississippian Period and are of very different, modern-looking animals. Gone are the trilobites, horn corals, crinoids, blastoids, most brachiopods, and most of the familiar kinds of Paleozoic marine life. Instead, we find a much greater variety of bivalves and gastropods and, for the first time, fish fossils are very common, especially sharks' teeth.

If one looks at a modern map of the coastline, it appears that its position is fixed and never changes. In fact, the coastline is constantly changing as sea level rises and falls and as the land is built up in some places and eroded away in others. During the entire Cenozoic Era, the coastline migrated back and forth across the Coastal Plain as the sea level changed. Sometimes, the ocean came right up to the edge of the present-day Piedmont. At other times, the sea was much lower, and the shoreline was many miles further east than it is today.

The first geologic division of the Cenozoic Era is known as the Tertiary Period. It is divided into five segments of time known as epochs. From oldest to youngest, these are the Paleocene, Eocene, Oligocene, Miocene, and Pliocene. At the end of the Pliocene Epoch, a little over a million and a half years ago, the Earth's climate became much colder. That event marks the beginning of the Ice Age and the start of the second Cenozoic period, known as the Quaternary Period. It is divided into two epochs, the Pleistocene and the Holocene.

During the Pleistocene Epoch, ice covering the area around the North Pole expanded in the form of glaciers and covered the northern parts of North America and Eurasia. The ice cover sometimes shrank in size and then grew again several times during the Pleistocene. The last time the glaciers grew smaller and retreated from the areas they had been covering was about 10,000 years ago. Scientists use that event to mark the beginning of the Holocene Epoch, which continues to the present day.

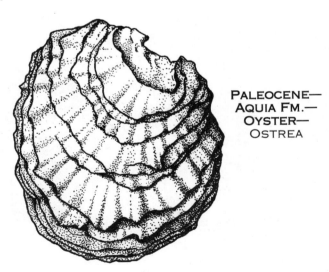

PALEOCENE—
AQUIA FM.—
OYSTER—
OSTREA

Chapter 17
Tertiary Period, Paleocene Epoch
65 to 58 million years ago

Paleocene fossils include a wide variety of mollusk and vertebrate remains. Some of the most interesting shell fossils are of large, cone-shaped gastropods known as *Turritellas*. In some places, sediments are packed full of *Turritellas*. Many bivalves may also be found, including numerous oysters, some of which grew to a very large size. The vertebrate remains from this epoch consist of abundant teeth of sharks, rays, and other fish, and the bones of crocodiles, birds, and large turtles.

Paleocene Marine Life

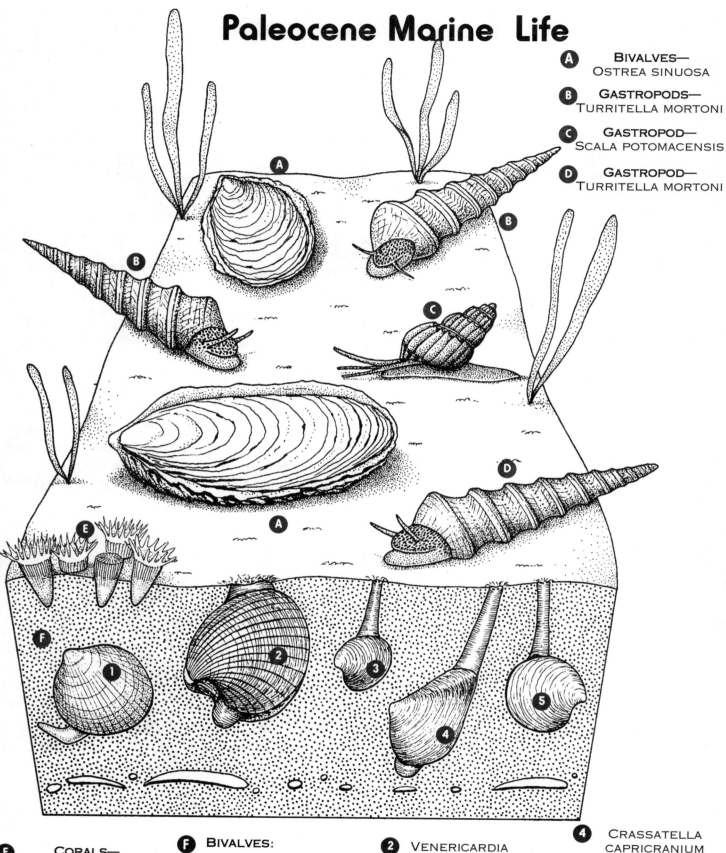

A **BIVALVES—** OSTREA SINUOSA

B **GASTROPODS—** TURRITELLA MORTONI

C **GASTROPOD—** SCALA POTOMACENSIS

D **GASTROPOD—** TURRITELLA MORTONI

E **CORALS—** EUPSAMMIA ELABORATA

F **BIVALVES:**

1 GLYCYMERIS

2 VENERICARDIA PLANICOSTA

3 PITAR OVATA

4 CRASSATELLA CAPRICRANIUM

5 DOSINIOPSIS LENTICULARIS

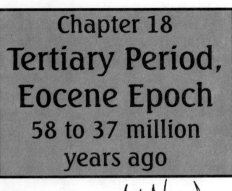

Chapter 18
Tertiary Period, Eocene Epoch
58 to 37 million years ago

Eocene fossils are less abundant than those from the Paleocene, but are mostly of the same kinds of animals, with a variety of bivalves and gastropods. *Turritellas* are still present but are smaller and less common than in the Paleocene sediments. One of the most abundant animals in the Eocene is the small bivalve known as *Venericardia*. In some places, up to 95% of the fossils are this species of **mollusk**. An interesting kind of mollusk found in the Eocene is known as *Cadulus.* This mollusk is found as a fossil throughout the Tertiary and is present today in marine settings.

Eocene Epoch
Nanjemoy Formation

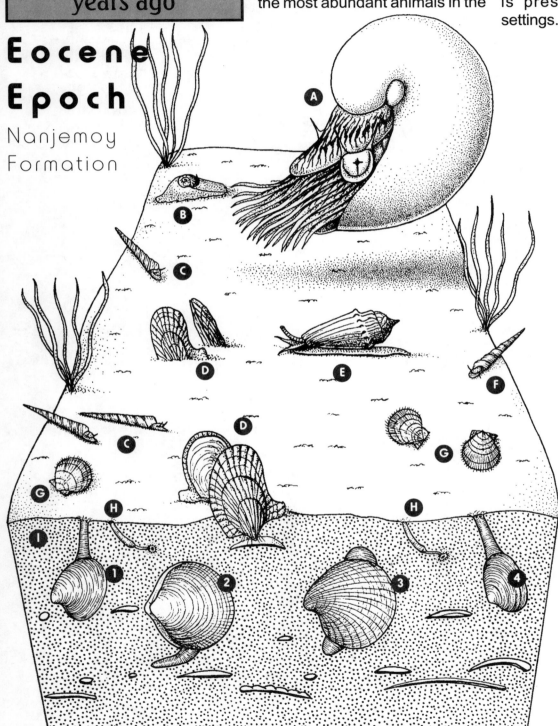

A NAUTILOID— HERCOGLOSSA SP.

B GASTROPOD— LUNATIA SP.

C GASTROPODS— TURRITELLA POTOMACENSIS

D BIVALVES— CUBITOSTREA SP.

E GASTROPOD— VOLUTILITHES PETROSUS

F GASTROPOD— TURRITELLA— POTOMACENSIS

G BIVALVES— PECTEN DALLI

H SCAPHOPOD— CADULUS SP.

I INFAUNAL BIVALVES:
1 MERETRIX OVATA
2 GLYCYMERIS IDONEUS
3 VENERICARDIA ASCIA
4 MACROCALLISTA SUBIMPRESSA

Miocene Marine Life: Sea Floor & Pelagic

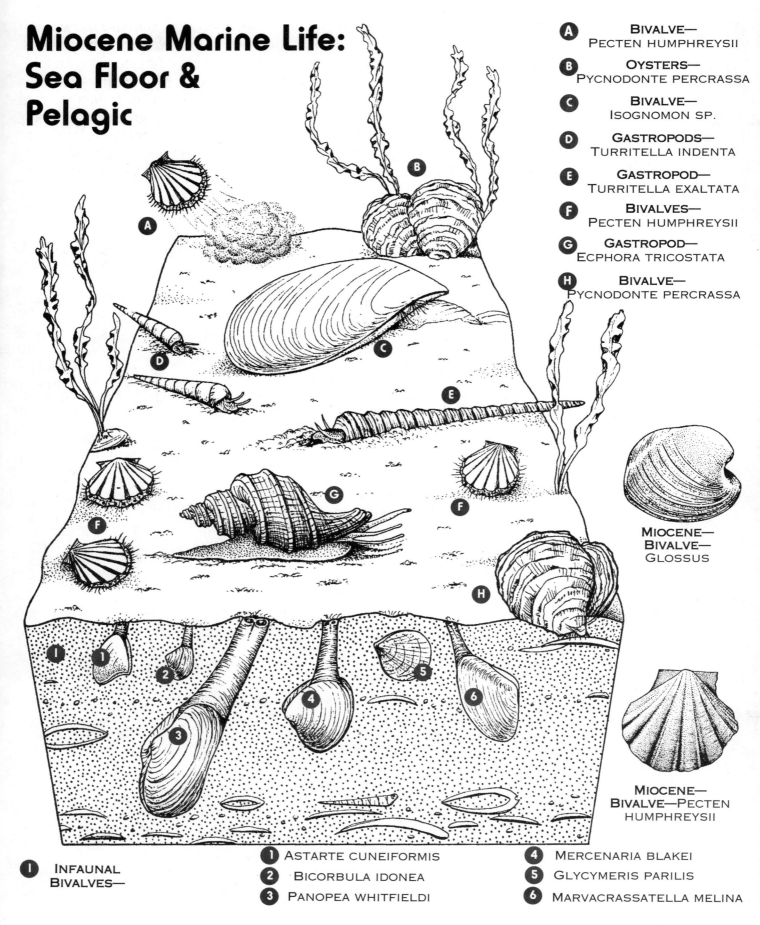

- **Ⓐ** BIVALVE— PECTEN HUMPHREYSII
- **Ⓑ** OYSTERS— PYCNODONTE PERCRASSA
- **Ⓒ** BIVALVE— ISOGNOMON SP.
- **Ⓓ** GASTROPODS— TURRITELLA INDENTA
- **Ⓔ** GASTROPOD— TURRITELLA EXALTATA
- **Ⓕ** BIVALVES— PECTEN HUMPHREYSII
- **Ⓖ** GASTROPOD— ECPHORA TRICOSTATA
- **Ⓗ** BIVALVE— PYCNODONTE PERCRASSA

MIOCENE— BIVALVE— GLOSSUS

MIOCENE— BIVALVE—PECTEN HUMPHREYSII

- **Ⓘ** INFAUNAL BIVALVES—
- **①** ASTARTE CUNEIFORMIS
- **②** BICORBULA IDONEA
- **③** PANOPEA WHITFIELDI
- **④** MERCENARIA BLAKEI
- **⑤** GLYCYMERIS PARILIS
- **⑥** MARVACRASSATELLA MELINA

Chapter 19
Tertiary Period, Oligocene and Miocene Epochs
37 to 5 million years ago

Oligocene fossils consist of a variety of *mollusks,* quite similar in type to those which may be found in the younger Miocene sediments. For this reason, and because their fossil record is so sketchy, we will look to the Miocene fossils to get an idea of what life was like at this time.

Virginia's Miocene fossils are world-famous for their variety, beautiful preservation, and abundance. The remains of a multitude of mollusks are present. In addition to crabs, there are **barnacles,** which are arthropods that attach themselves firmly to other structures. Echinoderms, corals, bryozoans, and even a few brachiopods are common. There are also many kinds of vertebrate fossils, including complete skeletons of whales, turtles, crocodiles, **manatees,** or "sea cows," which are a type of water-dwelling mammal, and the bones and teeth of fish such as sharks, rays, and swordfish. The teeth of one extinct Miocene shark, ***Carcharodon megalodon,*** may be 6 inches long, or even more. It is estimated that these sharks were as much as 50 feet long! The teeth and bones of Miocene terrestrial animals such as horses and elephant-like **gomphotheres** were sometimes swept out to sea. These remains were then buried in marine deposits and may be found among the fossils of sea creatures today.

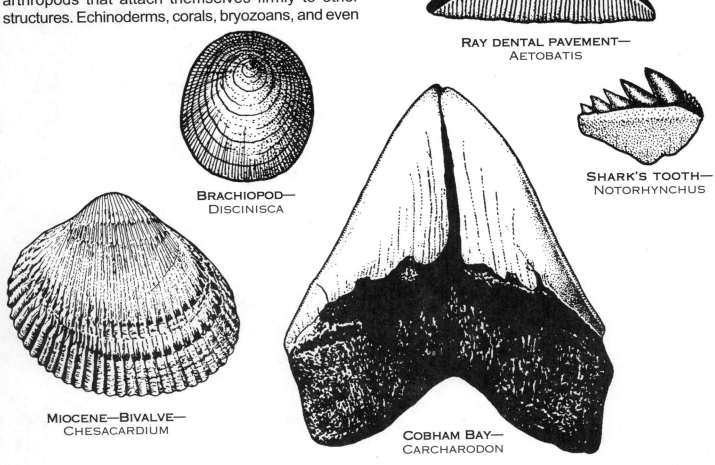

RAY DENTAL PAVEMENT—
AETOBATIS

BRACHIOPOD—
DISCINISCA

SHARK'S TOOTH—
NOTORHYNCHUS

MIOCENE—BIVALVE—
CHESACARDIUM

COBHAM BAY—
CARCHARODON

ROSTRUM—"SWORD" OF A
SWORDFISH

Mid-Atlantic Pliocene fossils are also renowned for their abundance and excellent preservation. Whale and shark remains are less common. The rich variety of mollusk fossils includes giant scallop shells, known as *Chesapecten*, which are often eight or nine inches in width. One of these, a species known as *Chesapecten jeffersonius,* has been designated as Virginia's official state fossil.

These giant scallops used to swim in schools of thousands, like today's deep sea scallops.

Also common in Pliocene sediments are large specimens of coral. These fossils tell scientists that Virginia's climate was slightly warmer during the Pliocene, because corals like these live in temperate waters.

Typical Pliocene Fossils

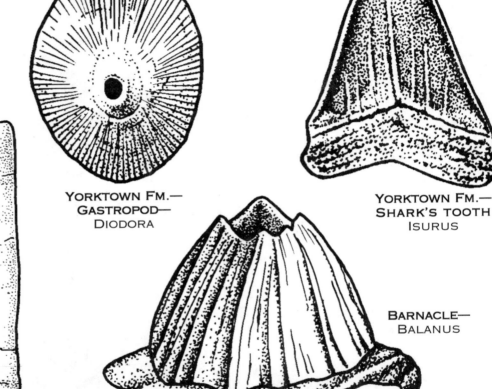

YORKTOWN FM.— GASTROPOD— DIODORA

YORKTOWN FM.— SHARK'S TOOTH ISURUS

YORKTOWN FM.— BIVALVE— KUPHUS

BARNACLE— BALANUS

YORKTOWN FM.— SHARK'S TOOTH— GALEOCERDO

YORKTOWN FM.— BRYOZOAN TETROCYCLOECIA

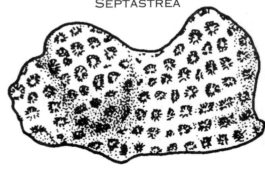

YORKTOWN FM.—CORAL— SEPTASTREA

38

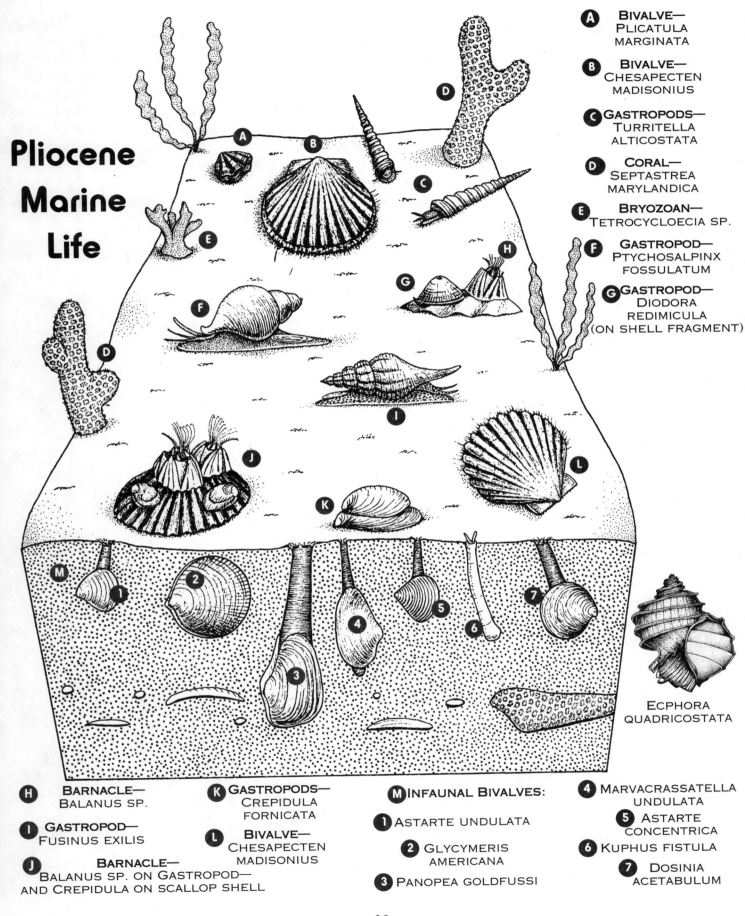

Pliocene Marine Life

A BIVALVE— PLICATULA MARGINATA

B BIVALVE— CHESAPECTEN MADISONIUS

C GASTROPODS— TURRITELLA ALTICOSTATA

D CORAL— SEPTASTREA MARYLANDICA

E BRYOZOAN— TETROCYCLOECIA SP.

F GASTROPOD— PTYCHOSALPINX FOSSULATUM

G GASTROPOD— DIODORA REDIMICULA (ON SHELL FRAGMENT)

ECPHORA QUADRICOSTATA

H BARNACLE— BALANUS SP.

I GASTROPOD— FUSINUS EXILIS

J BARNACLE— BALANUS SP. ON GASTROPOD— AND CREPIDULA ON SCALLOP SHELL

K GASTROPODS— CREPIDULA FORNICATA

L BIVALVE— CHESAPECTEN MADISONIUS

M INFAUNAL BIVALVES:

1 ASTARTE UNDULATA

2 GLYCYMERIS AMERICANA

3 PANOPEA GOLDFUSSI

4 MARVACRASSATELLA UNDULATA

5 ASTARTE CONCENTRICA

6 KUPHUS FISTULA

7 DOSINIA ACETABULUM

Chapter 21
Quaternary Period, Pleistocene Epoch
1.6 million 10,000 years ago

In the late Pliocene Epoch, and into the Pleistocene, the climate of the Mid-Atlantic region became much cooler. The northern polar ice cap, made of ice up to 10,000 feet thick, expanded and covered much more of the Earth's surface. As a result, more of the Earth's water was trapped in the form of ice, and sea level dropped considerably. That process resulted in fewer Pleistocene marine sediments and fossils. Still, Pleistocene remains of whales, sharks, gastropods and bivalves may be found in the southeastern corner of Virginia.

The terrestrial vertebrate fossils of the Pleistocene from deposits that accumulated along lakes and rivers are not common, but those found show the variety of animals that lived here during the so-called "Ice Age." Specimens include the remains of elephant-like mammoths and **mastodons,** hoofed animals called **tapirs**, bears, beavers, pig-like **peccaries, ground sloths,** deer, moose, horses, camels, and cattle-like **bison**. Even fossils of walruses and crocodiles have been discovered. The fact that so few of these animals still live here shows how much the climate has changed since the end of the Pleistocene.

Plant fossils, including petrified wood, leaves, pine cones, and even pecans, also occur in many parts of the mid-Atlantic region.

Typical Mid-Atlantic Pleistocene Fossils

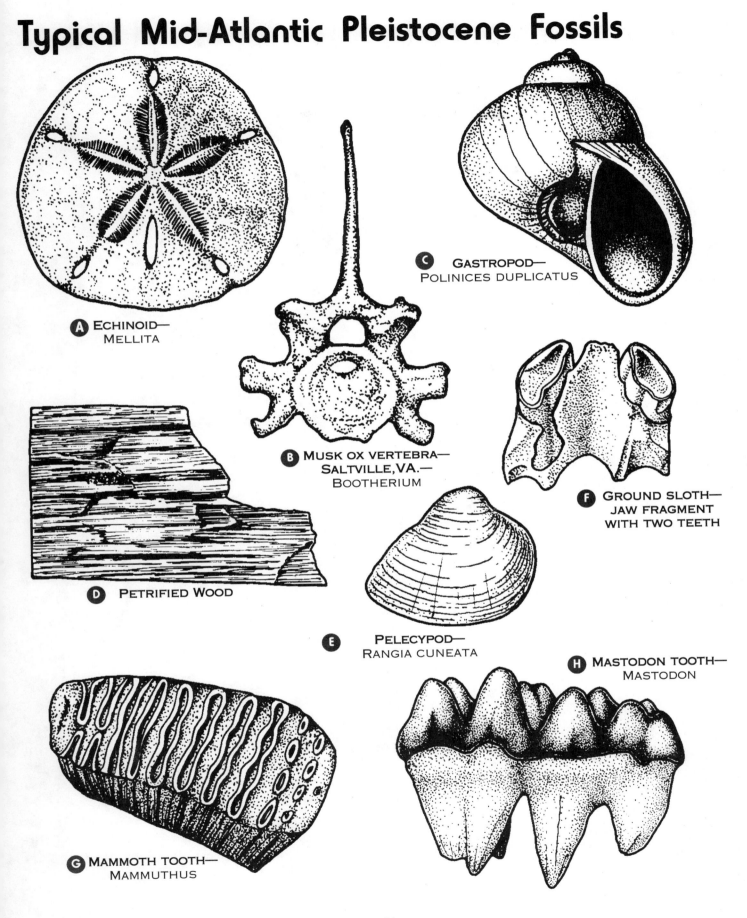

A ECHINOID—
MELLITA

B MUSK OX VERTEBRA—
SALTVILLE, VA.—
BOOTHERIUM

C GASTROPOD—
POLINICES DUPLICATUS

D PETRIFIED WOOD

E PELECYPOD—
RANGIA CUNEATA

F GROUND SLOTH—
JAW FRAGMENT
WITH TWO TEETH

G MAMMOTH TOOTH—
MAMMUTHUS

H MASTODON TOOTH—
MASTODON

41

Reconstruction of Pleistocene Terrestrial Life

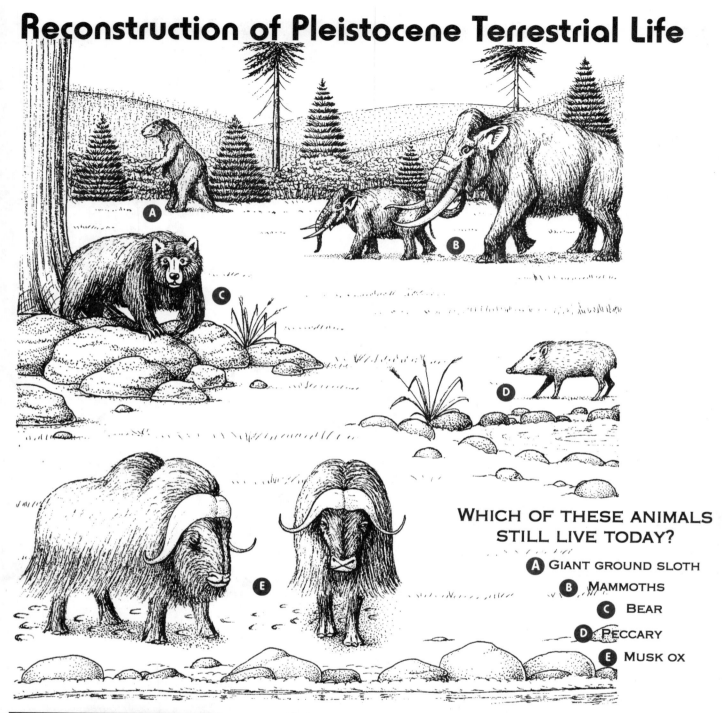

WHICH OF THESE ANIMALS STILL LIVE TODAY?

A GIANT GROUND SLOTH
B MAMMOTHS
C BEAR
D PECCARY
E MUSK OX

Chapter 22
Quaternary Period
Holocene Epoch
10,000 years ago to present day

There are many remains of plants and animals that lived in the Mid-Atlantic region since the end of the Pleistocene. These include old shells that are buried in sand dunes, and bones, logs, and other remains that are buried in soil. These traces are mostly of the kinds of plants and animals that live today. Scientists call them subfossils. But if they escape destruction and are discovered by paleontologists in the distant future, they will be studied as the fossils of life as it was during the Holocene Epoch of the Quaternary Period. They may seem as strange and wonderful to the scientists of the future as the fossils we know seem to us today.

Flashing Fossils

When scientists are working in the field it is helpful to recognize the common fossil groups and their associated ages. Can you recognize some common fossils by name and age? Cut out these flash cards along the dotted lines. Look at the pictures on the front of the card and try to remember the name of the plant or animal whose fossil you see. Use the book to check your answers. Write the name of the plant or animal and the era when it was usually found on the back of the cards. Now you have a set of flash cards. Quiz yourself and your friends to get prepared for hunting fossils in the field!

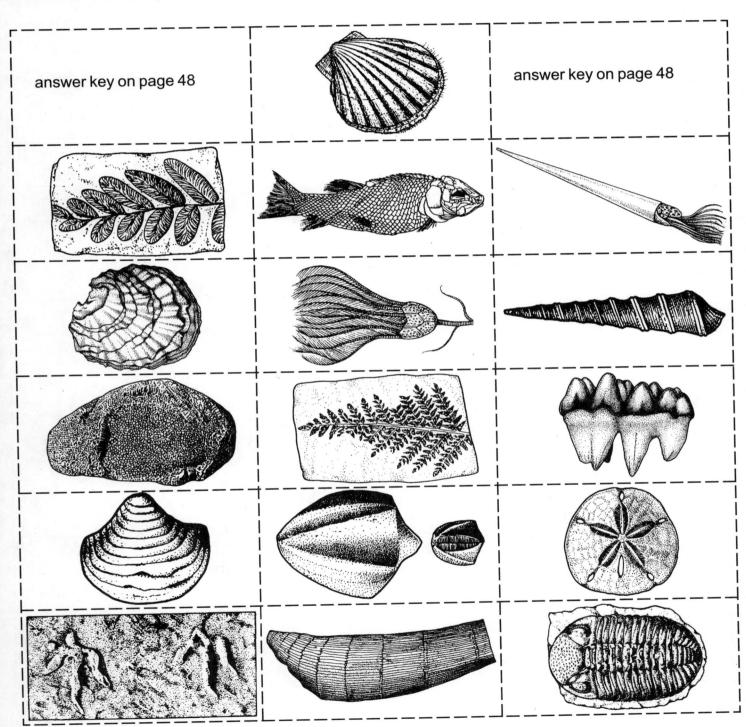

answer key on page 48

answer key on page 48

Paleo Detective

You are a lab assistant for a paleontologist at the Virginia Museum of Natural History. The team has just returned from the field and left you a set of fossils to be examined and classified. Examine each group of fossils and try to identify the geologic period they are from and some of their scientific names. Use the book and your flash cards to check your work.

Group 1: *Turritella, Carcharodon megalodon, Ostrea, Buccinofusus*

Group 2: *Olenellus, Kutorgina*, stromatolite, *Archaeocyathus*

Group 3: *Tanytrachelos*, water bug, cycad, *Semionotus*

Group 4: Mastodon tooth, musk ox vertebrae, petrified wood, ground sloth jaw

Flashing Fossils

Back of flash cards.

NAME ____________
ERA ____________

Paleo Detective
answer key
1. Tertiary Period
2. Cambrian Period
3. Triassic and Jurassic Period
4. Quarternary Period

NAME ____________
ERA ____________

NAME ____________
ERA ____________

NAME ____________
ERA ____________

NAME ____________
ERA ____________

NAME ____________
ERA ____________

NAME ____________
ERA ____________

NAME ____________
ERA ____________

NAME ____________
ERA ____________

NAME ____________
ERA ____________

NAME ____________
ERA ____________

NAME ____________
ERA ____________

NAME ____________
ERA ____________

NAME ____________
ERA ____________

NAME ____________
ERA ____________

NAME ____________
ERA ____________

The illustration below is a recreation of life from the Yorktown Formation showing *Chesapecten jeffersonius*. This picture includes many mollusks that lived in the sand near *Chesapecten jeffersonius*. Use the drawing below along with all of the previous information to help you make a drawing of this fossil as it lived in the Atlantic Ocean approximately 4.5 million years ago.

Use guide books to help give you more information about the other animals that lived with *Chesapecten*. Think carefully about where in the picture each of the animals would be found. Add color to make it more interesting.

Pliocene Epoch— Yorktown Formation

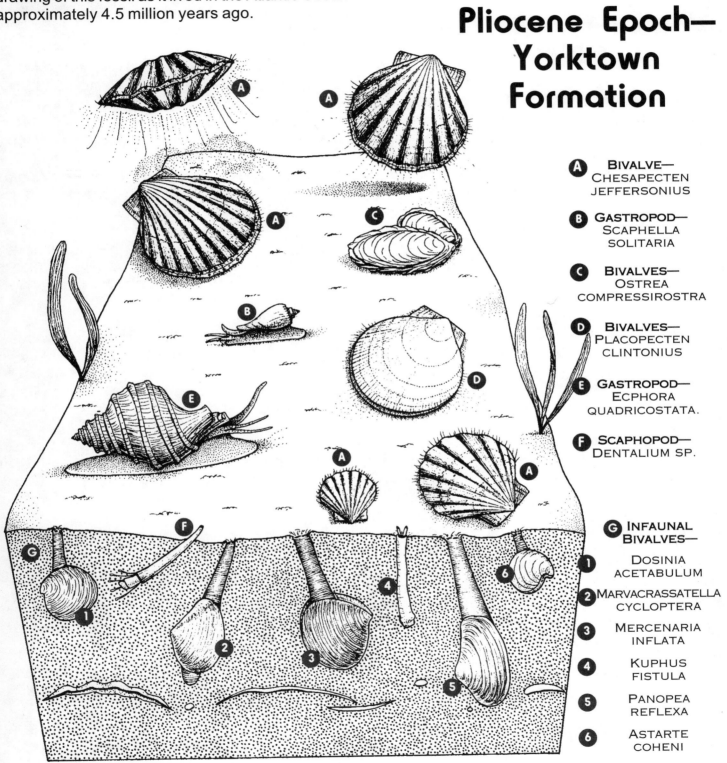

A BIVALVE— CHESAPECTEN JEFFERSONIUS

B GASTROPOD— SCAPHELLA SOLITARIA

C BIVALVES— OSTREA COMPRESSIROSTRA

D BIVALVES— PLACOPECTEN CLINTONIUS

E GASTROPOD— ECPHORA QUADRICOSTATA.

F SCAPHOPOD— DENTALIUM SP.

G INFAUNAL BIVALVES—

1 DOSINIA ACETABULUM

2 MARVACRASSATELLA CYCLOPTERA

3 MERCENARIA INFLATA

4 KUPHUS FISTULA

5 PANOPEA REFLEXA

6 ASTARTE COHENI

Did you know that Virginia, Pennsylvania, Maryland and West Virginia have state fossils? *Chesapecten jeffersonius* was officially named Virginia's state fossil in 1993. It was chosen because it was the first fossil ever described in North America. Also, it was named after Thomas Jefferson, a Virginian who was one of the early paleontologists of this country. It is found only in Virginia and a few locations in North Carolina. Take a look at the drawing of this fossil. What can you tell about this creature by looking at the fossil? You clearly know the size and shape of the creature, but where did it live? What did it eat? With what other animals and plants did this scallop interact? These are all questions paleontologists try to answer as they study fossils and the sediments in which they are found. In order to answer some of these questions, paleontologists look at living species of similar creatures and study their behavior and physical characteristics.

After reading the scientific information about *Chesapecten jeffersonius* and several other animals that lived in the sea near *Chesapecten*, try to draw a picture of the *Chesapecten* in an ocean off the coast of ancient Virginia.

Chesapecten jeffersonius was a giant sea scallop. Its fossils can be found in the Pliocene Yorktown Formation, which dates to 4.5 million years ago. It lived on clean, fine sand along the continental shelf at depths over 40-50 feet. *Chesapectens* did not attach themselves permanently to the bottom of the ocean. They were swimmers. These scallops probably swam in schools in the cool temperate waters of the Atlantic. Modern large scallops swim in a zig-zag motion by rapidly opening and closing their shells. Water is sucked into the front and rapidly forced back out again. Scientists have learned this by observing modern species of scallops. Younger *Chesapectens* usually do not have barnacles or other encrusting organisms on them, because they were very mobile. Larger, older specimens are found with sponge holes and barnacles attached, which indicates they were less active. Modern deep sea scallops have unusual vision. They have rows of steely gray eyes set along the edge of their shell opening,

which are sensitive to light and movement. It is probable that *Chesapecten* had such eyes. Some common shell colors of modern scallops are orange, purple, yellow, white, and brown. They often have interesting spotted color patterns on their shells.

What other animals lived with *Chesapecten* in the ancient Atlantic Ocean? This question has been answered by Dr. Lauck Ward, an invertebrate paleontologist at the Virginia Museum of Natural History who has studied the fossils of the Yorktown Formation, where *Chesapecten jeffersonius* fossils are abundant. Following is a list of some other animals found as fossils with *Chesapecten jeffersonius*. Many of these types of animals still exist today.

Carcharodon megalodon, an extinct giant shark. Teeth found from this shark have been up to 6 inches long, leading scientists to believe that these sharks reached up to 50 feet in length.

Balaena, a right whale, which still exists today. Right whales are baleen whales who use baleen plates in their mouths to filter out small creatures like krill from the water. The ear bones of these whales have unusual shapes and are often found as fossils.

Myliobatis, an eagle ray, which can be found in the Atlantic Ocean today. Modern eagle rays live in warm seas, close to sandy or muddy sea floors. They feed on mollusks, crustaceans, and small fish.

Septastrea, an extinct hexacoral that lived in the Atlantic Ocean during the Miocene and Pliocene Epochs. It lived in large, branching colonies.

Some other animals that left fossil remains in the sand near *Chesapecten* are blue whales, porpoises, sperm whales, swordfish, and sea turtles.

YORKTOWN FM.–CORAL–
SEPTASTREA

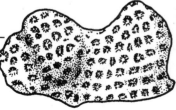

GLOSSARY

aeolian deposits—sediments accumulated through the action of wind.

algae—single plants with chlorophyll, most of which live in water.

archaeocyathids—extinct ocean-dwelling animals similar to sponges, common in the Cambrian Period.

arthropods—invertebrate animals with external shells and jointed body and legs.

bacteria—very simple one-celled organisms.

barnacles—marine crustaceans which attach themselves firmly to shells, rocks, or man-made structures.

bison—a hoofed, cattle-like mammal. The American buffalo is a bison.

bivalves—a class of mollusks which lives in fresh and salt water. Bivalves have two shells, usually of the same size, which fit tightly together to protect the soft animal inside.

blastoids—an extinct group of marine echinoderms which lived during the Paleozoic Era. Blastoids attached themselves to the sea bottom with a stalk.

brachiopods—a group of marine animals with two shells for protection. Unlike bivalves, brachiopods usually have shells of somewhat different sizes.

bryozoans—tiny water-living colonial animals which build structures housing many individuals in tiny chambers.

cast—an object formed when the hollow space in sediments left by the decompsed plant or animal remains is filled by minerals. A cast will be similar in shape to the original remains.

cephalopods—a group of marine mollusks which includes squids, nautiloids, the extinct ammonoids, and octopuses.

colony—a group of animals of one kind which live together permanently, often in special structures built cooperatively.

conifers—the large group of plants which produce seed-bearing structures known as cones. Pines, spruces, redwoods, and firs are familiar kinds of conifers.

corallites—the individual coral animals that make up a coral colony.

crinoid—an ocean-dwelling echinoderm. Most crinoids that are found as fossils were attached to the sea bottom by a long stalk, but many modern forms have no stalk.

crustaceans—the group of arthropods that includes crabs, barnacles, and shrimps.

cycads—a kind of plant with scaly trunks and palm-like leaves that was very common during the Mesozoic Era. Cycads still live today, but are much less common.

cynodonts—an extinct group of reptiles that lived during the Permian and Triassic periods. Their skeletons resemble the skeletons of mammals so they are sometimes called "mammal-like reptiles." Mammals are believed to have developed from a kind of cynodont.

cystoids—an extinct group of echinoderms which lived in the ocean during the Paleozoic Era.

echinoderms—a large group of invertebrate marine animals including starfish, sea cucumbers, and sand dollars.

exposure—a place where rocks may be seen at the surface of the earth, rather than being buried under soil or other materials.

extinct—no longer living. Refers to a group or species that has died out.

ferns—See true ferns.

formation—A traceable body of rock that is internally consistent and recognizable.

gastropods—a large group of mollusks, most of which possess coiled shells and are known as snails.

gomphotheres—an extinct kind of elephant-like mammal.

graptolites - an extinct group of marine invertebrates that lived in floating colonies during the Paleozoic Era.

ground sloths—an extinct group of ground-dwelling mammals related to the modern tree sloth. Some ground sloths grew to the size of elephants during the Ice Age.

horn corals—an extinct kind of coral. They are called horn corals because they formed curved cone-shaped structures that resemble the horns of animals such as cows.

horsetails—a group of plants which includes some very large types such as *Calamites*, that lived in the forests of the Pennsylvanian Period. Horsetails still live today, but are relatively small.

hyolithids—an extinct group of marine invertebrates that lived during the Paleozoic Era. They may have been related to mollusks.

GLOSSARY

igneous rocks—rocks that were formed from molten or liquid rock such as lava.

infaunal—living in a soft sea bottom.

invertebrates—animals that do not have backbones.

lycopsids—a group of plants that includes the scale trees which grew to enormous size in the forests of the Pennsylvanian Period. A few, very small lycopsids live today.

mammoths—extinct close relatives of the elephants.

manatees—also known as "sea cows." Manatees live in water and look something like seals. One kind of manatee lives in bays and rivers in Florida today.

marine—living in sea water.

mastodons—extinct relatives of elephants.

metamorphic rocks—rocks that have been drastically changed in their internal structure by extreme heat or pressure. Metamorphic rocks may have been either igneous rocks *or* sedimentary rocks originally.

mold—the hollow space left when an object that is buried in sediments, such as a shell or bone, decays or is dissolved away. If this space is filled over time by minerals a *cast* is formed.

mollusks—a large group of invertebrate animals that includes bivalves, gastropods, scaphopods, and cephalopods.

nautiloids—the group of cephalopods that includes the living "pearly nautilus" and numerous extinct forms found as fossils. Nautiloids are a kind of mollusk.

peccaries—a form of wild pig common today.

phytosaurs—a group of extinct reptiles that resembled crocodiles in appearance.

scale trees—extinct plants belonging to the group known as lycopsids. They grew in the forests of the Pennsylvanian Period.

scaphopods—a group of marine mollusks, sometimes called "tusk shells" which have curved, hollow shells with an opening at each end.

sediment—the mud and sand that settle to the bottom under bodies of water.

sedimentary rocks—rocks that are formed when sediments are turned to stone by pressure or certain chemicals. Some kinds of sedimentary rocks are shale, sandstone, and limestone.

seed ferns—a kind of plant whose leaves often resemble those of true ferns. Unlike true ferns, they reproduce by means of seeds rather than spores.

spiriferids—an extinct kind of brachiopod whose shells often have a central fold with rib-like ridges on either side.

spore—a reproductive structure made by true ferns and other primitive plants which, unlike seeds, consists of only one cell each.

stromatolites—layered sedimentary structures made through the action of blue-green algae and bacteria. Stromatolites were common in the Pre-Cambrian Era and still survive today on the coast of Australia and in fresh water.

tapirs—a kind of hoofed mammal related to horses and rhinoceroses.

tentaculitids—an extinct group of marine invertebrates which had cone-shaped shells.

theropods—the large group of meat-eating dinosaurs which includes *Tyrannosaurus rex* and many smaller species.

trilobites—a large extinct group of marine arthropods. Their fossils are very common in rocks from the early Paleozoic Era, but they disappeared at the end of the Permian Period.

true ferns—a group of plants, many of which have complex leaves made up of many small leaflets. Unlike many other kinds of plants, they use spores rather than seeds to reproduce.

vertebrates—animals with backbones.

dinosaur track *theropod dinosaur* Mesozoic	horsetail *Calamites* Paleozoic	trilobite *Phacops* Paleozoic
brachiopod *Kutorgina* Paleozoic	blastoid *Pentremites* Paleozoic	sand dollar *Mellita* Cenozoic
coral *Favosites* Paleozoic	fern *Osmunda* Cenozoic and Mesozoic	mastodon tooth *Mammut* Cenozoic
oyster *Ostrea* Cenozoic	crinoid *Arthroacantha* Paleozoic	gastropod *Turritella* Cenozoic and Mesozoic
seed fern *Neuropteris* Paleozoic	fish *Semionotus* Mesozoic	nautiloid *Michelinoceras* Paleozoic
	scallop *Chesapecten jeffersonius* Cenozoic	